RESCUING AFRICAN MARRIAGES IN THE DIASPORA

Abraham Kicha

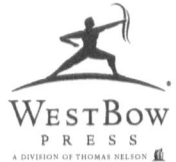

WestBow
PRESS
A DIVISION OF THOMAS NELSON

WestBow Press books may be ordered through booksellers or by contacting:

WestBow Press
A Division of Thomas Nelson
1663 Liberty Drive
Bloomington, IN 47403
www.westbowpress.com
1-(866) 928-1240

ISBN: 978-1-4497-6594-1 (sc)
ISBN: 978-1-4497-6595-8 (e)

Library of Congress Control Number: 2012920605

Printed in the United States of America

WestBow Press rev. date: 11/07/2012

Dedication

With lots of thanksgiving unto God the Father, God the Son , God the Holy Spirit, I dedicate this book to the following

My beloved father late Bobe David Cheng. As a little boy I saw and learned from his loving kindness towards women who came from far away villages to have their babies at Belo maternity. These women never informed him that they were coming. It was not the nearness of his house to the maternity that attracted these women, but his love and Christ –like hospitality that attracted them. Some he did not know their names and could only call them " wain-nawain." He remains my hero and life model. May his soul rest in peace.

My beloved father late Bobe Manfred Kicha who schooled me on the importance of loving my wife. May his soul rest in peace.

My beloved mother-in-law late Nawain Margret Nain. Sometimes I call my wife by her name because of the love she had for me. I pray to remain a good husband to her daughter and a good father to her grandsons as she requested the last day a met her in the hospital in Douala. May her soul rest in peace

My beloved sister, late Elizabeth Kicha. She was a wonderful sister and friend who was in deep love with my wife. May her soul rest in peace.

My beloved sister late Evelyn Kicha who lived with me when I was still single and was of great help to me. May her soul rest in peace.

My beloved in-law late Bobe Francis Ful who covered my wife and I when rain was falling on us and loved me as a son. May his soul rest in peace.

Contents

Introduction

A title like this one usually rings many bells in the mind of whoever comes across it. It takes time, pain, and money to rescue something or someone trapped in a dangerous situation. God had to become man in order to rescue humanity, which he created in his image, from the power of sin and death. With the help of television, I have seen lots of heartbreaking rescue efforts.

- The rescue of thirty-three Chilean miners trapped two thousand feet underground for more than two months caught the attention of all who watched it.
- A man in New York left his two little daughters by the roadside to rescue a stranger who collapsed on a railway as a train approached. He lay on top of the man as the train passed probably two inches above his back. This was high risk. Thank God, he rescued the man, and both were not hurt.
- The mayor of Newark came home on the night of Thursday, April 12, 2012, and found his neighbor's house was on fire. He immediately rushed in and helped rescue the woman through life-threatening flames and smoke.
- Two brothers died in Lake California trying to rescue a dog, and rescue workers in California struggled to rescue a drowning dog. Many Africans would see the loss of life in the struggle to rescue a dog as madness.

Marriage also needs to be rescued. The importance of marriage to any community can never be overemphasized. "Marriage is honorable in all, and the bed undefiled: but whoremongers and adulterers God will judge" (Heb. 13:4). Marriage is the foundation of all communities and nations. Strong and stable marriages produce strong communities, stable nations, and churches. "If the foundations be destroyed, what can the righteous do?" (Ps. 11:3).

Marriage, a God-ordained institution, is a lifelong relationship between one man and one woman. As the two live together under the heat and pressures of life, they get lost in each other to the point it is impossible to tell where one ends and the other begins. Marriage is a process, a fusion of two distinct elements into one sparkling jewel of love, faithfulness, and commitment that shines brightly in a world of short lives and impermanence.[1]

William R. Cunningham says, "In the Christian perspectives, marriage is more than just the union of two Christians of the opposite sex. A Christian marriage is characterized and governed by Christian principles that are taught in the Bible. Christian marriage adheres to the standards of marriage revealed in the Holy Bible." All around the world, across all religions and cultures, successful societies have been those based on strong marriages.[2]

As it was in the beginning, God the creator intended that marriage should be a lifetime covenant relationship between one man and one woman. In the West, it is called "traditional marriage." God's decree cannot be reduced to the level of a mere tradition handed down to us from generation to generation. When those of us from Africa and other continents hear of "traditional marriage," in our minds, it has nothing to do with divine declaration. Even though there may be references to polygamy in the Bible, polygamy does not have a divine declaration. The practice stems from our fallen human nature, which God allowed, but he does not decree it in the Bible. The more the West calls marriage between one man and one woman traditional marriage, the harder it is for an African theologian or pastor to defend the fact that Christianity is not just a white man's religion and tradition.

In a good marriage, partners complement each other and make both better. Marriage, a journey through life, enhances and enriches entire communities. Lack of marriage is the death of a nation and a people. Communities that fail to recognize marriage become decadent and self-destructive with a range of social, economic, and health issues. Marriage is sacred in Africa and elsewhere, because it solidifies relationships that enrich communities and nations by bringing forth new life and new hope.[3]

---

[1]   Myles Munroe, *The Purpose and Power of Marriage* (Shippensburg, Pa.: Destiny Image Publishers, Inc., 2002), 21.

[2]   J. D. Unwin, *Sex and Culture* (Oxford: Oxford University Press, 1934), 431.

[3]   *www.africanholocaust.net/news_ah/africanmarriageritual.html.*

But marriages are in trouble all over the world. Even in Africa, many marriages are going through difficult times. But when I compare African marriages on the African continent and those in the diaspora, I see African marriages in the diaspora are going through hell. When I was pastoring in Africa, I heard the foundation of African marriages in the diaspora was broken. I did not know the magnitude until, by the grace of God, I joined other Africans in the diaspora. Now I have seen the storms raging against African marriages in the diaspora. I have heard living, painful testimonies about the strain on African marriages outside the continent. My own marital foundation has been shaken. If my marriage were not built on Christ, the only solid foundation, it would have been a different story today.

I set out to learn more about what African marriages were going through. I knew something needed to be done to help these struggling marriages. I thought if I presented all I heard about African marriages in the diaspora they might be helped. When I decided to write, I could not find one book that contained anything about the plight of African marriages in the diaspora. I went to the Internet and found concrete information concerning the desperate state of African marriages in the diaspora, which I present in the first chapter of this book. It tells about the shattered foundation of Africans marriages in the diaspora. If you put together what you read here with what you have seen, heard, and experienced, you will find that this book is a glimpse at these marriages. This book does not offer a complete solution, but it opens your eyes to what is destroying our marriages. If you ask my wife or I what was wrong with our marriage, neither of us would have an answer. Our pastor friend Johnson, who was with us, did not understand what was going on. Sometimes I think it was spiritual, and I may be right. It takes the determination of a couple—the husband and wife—to rescue a sinking marriage and to maintain a healthy union. They have to pray and do what is necessary to rescue their marriage.

Rescue workers may rush into houses and save people trapped inside. They may rescue drowning persons and dogs on the high seas, but not one can save a sinking marriage. The man and woman involved must rescue any trouble marriage. If they want to fix their marriage and fall in love again—or for the first time—they can do it. No outsider can do it for any family. Information in this book and others on this subject can help only those who are serious in making a difference in their marriage.

The safety of any marriage lies solely in the hands of the husband and wife making good use of the material their pastor or marriage counselor presents to them or what they find in books.

- If you are married, I pray you find help in this book that will sweeten your union.
- If you are single, I pray that as you read this book, you will not make the same mistakes as many of your friends.
- If your marriage is already on the rocks, I pray God will help you in your struggle to save your marriage or prevent your union from taking a downward turn.

Who should get a copy of this book?

- Every African family living in the diaspora
- Each African family in the diaspora with young adults, giving a copy to each
- All African congregations or churches in the diaspora, giving a copy to each member and using in a Sunday or Bible class
- Each Western pastor or church with an African family in its congregation, providing the pastor with an understanding of what African marriages in his community face

CHAPTER 1

Face to Face with Plight:
African Marriages in the Diaspora

These are true stories of what Africans in the diaspora are going through. I did not want to write just what I heard. Thank God I did not get the reports from a book you may not have access to. I got these stories from the Internet, and anyone is free to check them. I just present a few so you get a better idea of what we are talking about. You can find more reports on African marriages in the diaspora on the Internet, stories exist that did not reach the media.

The African nations represented in these reports are not the only ones whose people experience troubled marriages in the diaspora. They are the only ones I could get stories about on the Internet. Yet they represent us all as Africans in the diaspora.

I would have preferred to present the stories to you as they appeared on the Internet. Since I could not obtain permission from the authors, I had to paraphrase the stories, making sure to stay as close as possible to the original. We will begin with Kenya, the giant of East Africa.

Troubled Kenyan Marriages in the Diaspora

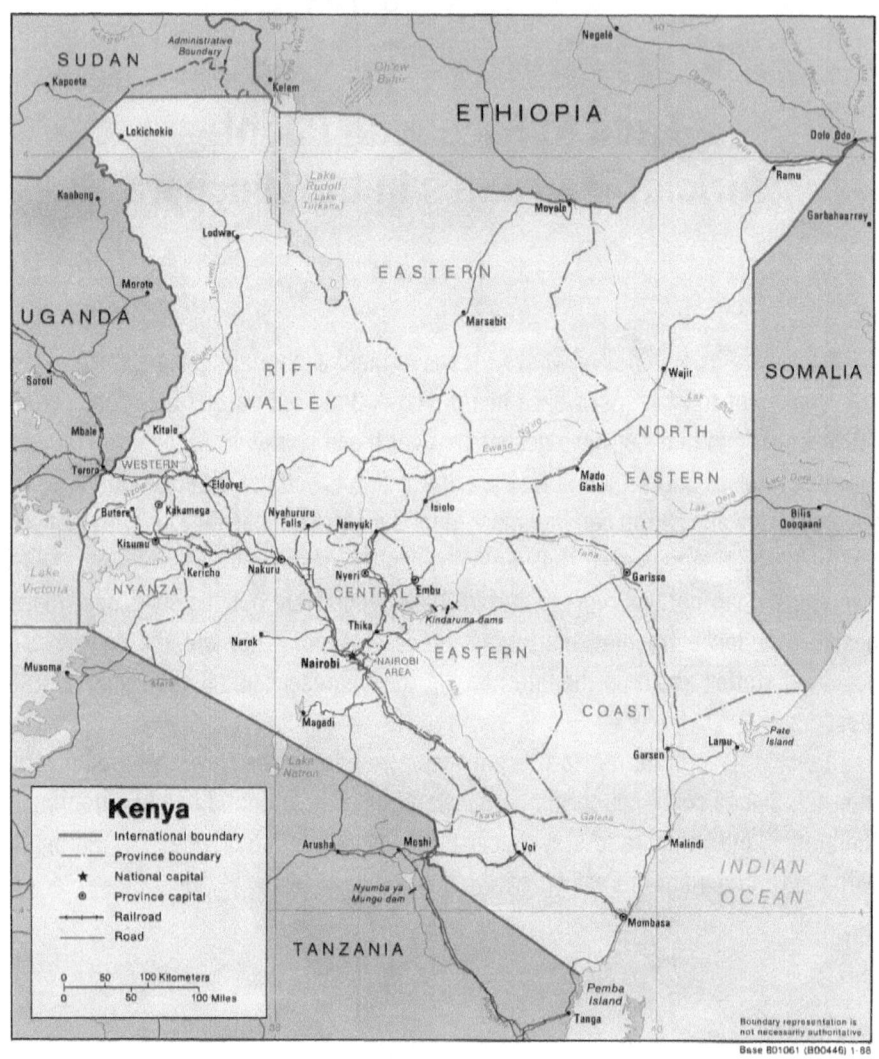

Pray for Kenya, pray for Africa

Kenya got her name from Mount Kenya. History also holds that, before the settlers arrived in this region, the Masai cattlemen and their wives and children dominated the area now known as Kenya. Later, the Arabs came looking for ivory. The Portuguese came and dismantled the Arabs, making way for the German missionaries to come to Kenya. Then the colonial masters passed through Zanzibar to colonize the whole region. Bismarck, having gotten up late in the quest for land in Africa, seized Zanzibar by force from its king. Britain had been there for a while, and already having enough in her basket, chose to share the region with Germany instead of picking up arms against the Kenyans. Fighting between the colonial masters might have given the struggling nationals the chance to regroup and regain their land. The Mau Mau fighters gave Britain no rest until it was forced to surrender Kenya to the Kenyans. On December 12, 1963, Kenya got her independence from Britain, and Jomo Kenyatta, a Kikuyu, became her first president.

Kenyans are lovely, hardworking people, with clearly defined tribal lines. This often leads to trouble in the land, and many Kenyans have moved to the diaspora. There they often work two or three jobs.

Reports of divorce, domestic unrest, and killings among Kenyans families in the diaspora, especially in America, have reached unspeakable rates. The site I visited also reports that uncountable Kenyan men are mercilessly hitting, and sometimes killing, their wives with objects you and I could not believe would be used on any living person.

Kenyans throughout diaspora are no longer ignoring the situation. They are asking questions about what has befallen them. The cries of Kenyans in the United States have reached the ears of the wife of the Kenyan ambassador to the United States. She has promised to address the issue wherever Kenyans are meeting in the United States as part of her own efforts to put an end to this brutality among Kenyan men and women.

For many, marriage, which used to be the glory of Africans and Kenyans in the diaspora, has become a shameful institution, and Kenyans are now speaking out. The pains of divorce and separations, and couples ending up in jails, are disgracing Africans in the diaspora.

The site goes no to enumerate some of the things Kenyans struggle with in the diaspora. These things often lead to divorce cases among Kenyans. The issues include:

financial problems

struggles with job schedules and the difficulty of balancing work and family
responsibilities

commitment to church activities

difficulty of raising children in the diaspora[4]

At a convention in November 2011, in Dallas, Texas, Kenyans sought to address the issues breaking apart their marriages in the diaspora. One of the speakers said there are multiple reasons Kenyans marriages are failing, and one of them is that Kenyans in the diaspora no longer view marriage as a divine institution. Kenyans who had always respected the institution of marriage now treat it like a mere social contract. Surprisingly, Kenyans now ask themselves what their profit will be if they marry a particular man or woman. They enter marriage with conflicting expectations, which end up giving birth to major conflicts that soon overpower their ability to endure. The marriage falls like a house built on sand.

A Kenyan clinical psychologist living in Florida has his theories why Kenyans marriages in the diaspora are falling apart. He says one of the reasons is that African men and women in the diaspora think widely differently from each other. These differences help the Kenyan woman advance in her career. The Kenyan man keeps regretting the state of things in the diaspora. As his regrets grow, the woman works harder and harder, and she soon achieves financial security, which only adds to the problems and fears the man has to bear. The Kenyan woman easily integrates herself in the diaspora by getting into the health-care sector, while the Kenyan man keeps marking time in one spot, wondering how he can go to school and learn a new career or how he can pick up a security job or work in a warehouse.

The psychologist goes on to say the concept of both partners in a couple being equal is foreign to the Kenyans, and to African culture as a whole. In Kenyan and other African cultures, there are things to be done only by women, and some to be done only by men. In Africa, men have nothing to do with most or all of domestic work; in the diaspora, they are often expected to share such responsibilities. In the Western world, women are heavily protected, with lots of rights. This is also unheard of in most African cultures.

---

[4] *www.mwakilishi.com/content/blogs/2011/05/27/what-is-ailing-diaspora-marriages.html*
7/19/11.

Many African men find it very difficult to accept this Western worldview, where laws seem to favor women and strip African man of rights he enjoyed in Africa. As African men seem to dangle in front of the Western law, African women use the laws to have their feet strongly rooted in the new, favored, Western culture.

In the diaspora, African women feel better treated than the African tradition treated them. In the diaspora, a married woman is expected to contribute financially to the upkeep of the family. Bills are often shared between the husband and wife. As the woman shares responsibilities of the household with her husband, she soon feels it is her right to share in the authority of running the household, something Kenyan men do not want to share with their wives. The wife's questioning the leadership position of the man in the family leads to many of the problems African marriages in the diaspora face. There is a general cry for the need to seek ways through which Africans in the diaspora can address these and other issues that cause so many marriages to fall apart.[5]

Another website I visited talks about a Kenyan couple that moved to the diaspora with their two children. In the diaspora, the wife soon found out that life demands both adults must work very hard to see their dreams come true. She soon got a job as a caregiver, while her husband still daydreamed. Due to his pride, he was unable to get a job as quickly as his wife did, but he later got a full-time job in a department store.

The hardworking Kenyan woman realized her income as a caregiver, combined with her husband's income, was not enough to handle their expenses in the diaspora and those at home in Kenya. So she took a bold step and enrolled in college part time while working full time. She also takes care of their two kids. She takes them to school in the morning before she goes to work, while her husband picks them up in the evening after his own work. Picking up the children from school and helping them with their homework are all the husband has offered to do for his family.

1. He sees cleaning, cooking, or any domestic household work as taboo. In his mind, such tasks have always been the responsibility of the woman.
2. His wife comes home from work, prepares meals for the family, and cleans the house before leaving for her class.
3. After school, she comes home to dirty dishes waiting for her in the sink, while her husband comfortably watches TV.

---

[5]   *www.area254.com/index.php/eng/Politics/Opinion/Opinions/opinion-new/Diaspora-.*

4. She is always the last person to go to bed and the first to get up early in the morning to continue with her unending daily activities.

As she interacts with friends at work and at school, she soon finds out most men in the West do help their wives with domestic work. She pleads with her husband to help her with some of the kitchen and housework. He refuses and tries to keep life just as it was in Africa.

5. The wife begins to see the man as heartless and inconsiderate, and the doors and windows of the house are opened for more troubles to come in.
6. This once-upon-a-time happy marriage ends up in a very bitter divorce.

If this causes divorce among Kenyans in the diaspora, we can call on Kenyan men to sit up and stop pushing their wives to the wall. It will then be well with them.[6]

*   *   *

A Kenyan woman and two of her kids where found dead in their Vadnais Heights apartment. The husband and the father of the two kids later confessed to the police that he is guilty of the crime. Their three-year-old son was with him in good condition. The police were still to make known the names of the deceased woman and her two kids, who were between nine and twelve years old. The police officer investigating the crime told reporters they went to the building to check on the safety of the people in that apartment. To their surprise, they found the bodies and clear evidence they were murdered. The suspect was not immediately found. The concern over the family arose when the woman had not reported at work for a week, and the children had not been in school for some days. Though not sure as to when the mother and her children died, investigators think she might have been murdered earlier in the week, and the children were later forced to join their mother in the land of the dead. The bodies were in different rooms; the woman's body was found in the bathroom.

---

[6] *http://diasporamessenger.com/index.php?option=com_k2&view=item&id=730:diaspora-marriages-change-needed&Itemid=1&lang=en.*

As it is said in America, "You can run, but you can't hide." The suspect was tracked down by Minnesota police.[7]

*   *   *

Another site I visited stated that US officials were struggling to reach relatives of a Kenyan woman believed to have been murdered. The woman, found dead in her apartment in Minnesota, was known by her close friends as Maurlyn Moore. It was reported that the deceased was from Mombasa, where she used to run a bridal shop. The deceased Kenyan woman was married to a Liberian. When the deceased came to the United States, she picked up a nursing job before marrying the Liberian man, who is a plumber. The police suspect she was murdered by her husband over what they say were marital issues. On the night of Tuesday, police were informed of a domestic unrest. When they got to the scene, they found a woman dead. Even though her names were not all gotten it is said that she came from Western Kenya. We are not told why it was difficult to get her names.

The suspect was booked and taken to the medical center for treatment of wounds he got from the conflict that led to the death of the woman.[8]

*   *   *

Kenyan Man Held in UK for "Raping" His Wife

Mr. Joseph Ngugi reports on one of the sites that UK police arrested a Kenyan charged with raping his wife. The man was on his way to Kenya when the UK police pulled him out of a flight bound for Nairobi, Kenya, at Heathrow Airport.

The man being bailed out of jail by one of his friends, said he spent about twenty hours in the Basildon, Essex, jail, where the Heathrow police had transferred him. Suspecting he might flee, police confiscated his passport and ordered him to return on January 22 the following year to hear if he will be charged. Basildon police told reporters they were investigating the alleged rape but refused to comment further on the case.

---

[7]   *www.jambonewspot.com.*

[8]   *www.africanoutlookonline.com/index.php?option=com_content&view=article&id=2872*
      :liberian-man-kills-kenyan-wife-in-minnesota-claims-self-defence&catid=29:courts-a-
      crime&Itemid=53.

The man, in a struggle to clear his name, told *News* reporters his wife raised the false rape alarm when he confronted her about her extramarital affair. In the United Kingdom, the law makes it very clear that a man can be convicted for raping his wife. Even though he denies the rape allegation, and there may be no witnesses, his fate lies in the hands of the judges in the court of law.

The couple, blessed with two sons, eight and five years old, have been married since 2000. The husband had been in London without his family for some time, while the wife was living in poverty in Kenya. After a long struggle, he succeeded in having his family join him in London about two years ago. The man says his marriage was a little heaven on earth when his wife joined him in London, but things turned bad when he lost his job as a youth worker with Basildon Council. Even though his wife also accused him of excessive drinking, the man thinks it is their financial hardship that caused the problems in their marriage.[9]

---

[9] *www.standardmedia.co.ke/archives/columnists/InsidePage.php?id=2000047577&cid=15 9&currentPage=1.*

Zimbabwean Troubled Marriages in the Diaspora

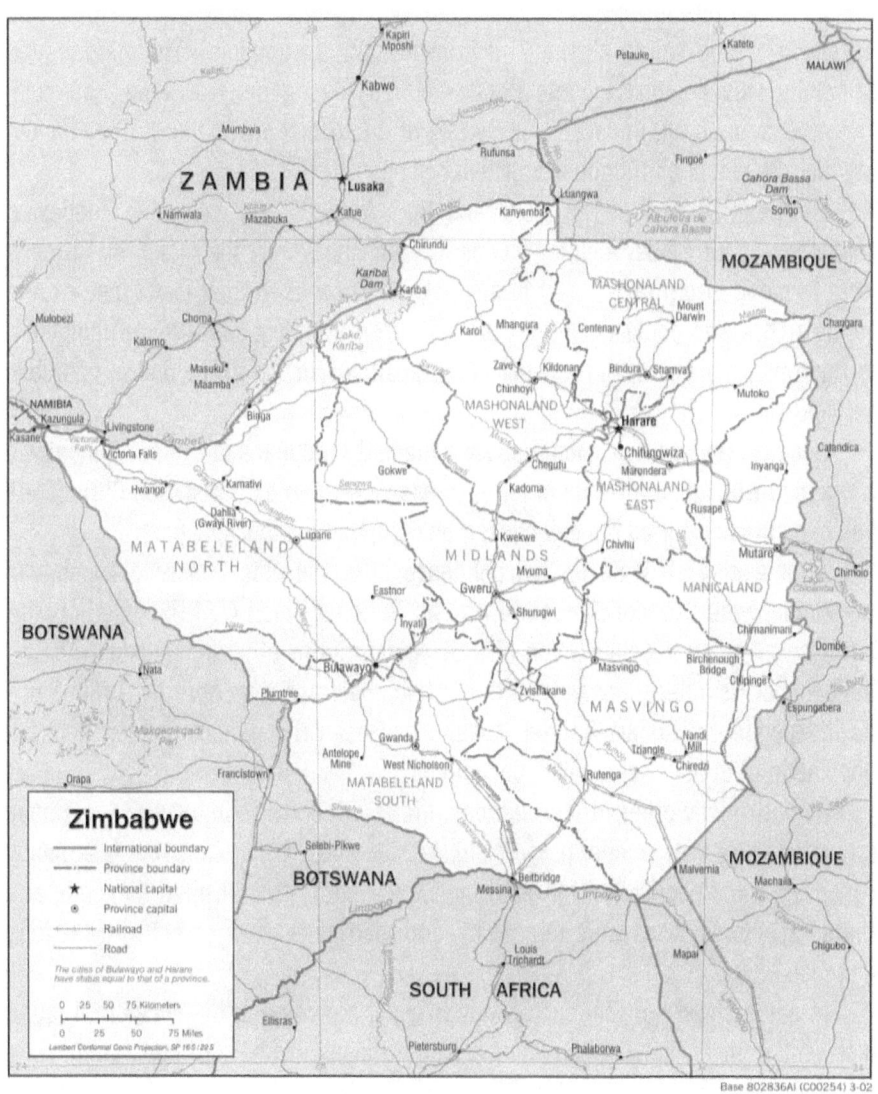

Pray for Zimbabwe, pray for Africa

Zimbabwe got its name from a pyramid that was built about AD 800-1500. It is the second-largest African pyramid, after those in Egypt. In the 1800s, Christian missionaries, the first Europeans to come to Zimbabwe, befriended King Mzilikazi for evangelistic purposes.

European businessmen without any religious agenda came after the Christian missionaries and seized all the land from Africans at gunpoint. The main leader, British businessperson Cecil John Rhodes, bought mining land from King Lobengula, and after some time, he and his army fought and overthrew the king. They named the land Rhodesia and made it a British colony.

European settlers seized more land from Africans and gave it to Rhodesian soldiers, who were busy killing Africans without mercy over their land. All Africans were forbidden from taking part in any political process in their land. They had no voting rights and could not stand for parliamentary elections. African indigents, in their own homeland, did not hold high positions in the army, police, or public service.

Because Christian missionaries were the first Europeans to come to Zimbabwe, white men who came after them for business were seen as Christians. Christianity has been blamed for all the evil caused by European businesspeople.

After a long struggle for independence after the defeat of King Lobengulo, the Zimbabweans, under Zimbabwe African National Union (ZANU), together with Zimbabwe African People's Union (ZAPU), supported by other independent African nations, got its independence from the British government on April 18, 1980. Since its independence, Robert Gabriel Mugaba has been the nation's leader. It has a population of about twelve million people.

As with many other African nations, life is difficult in Zimbabwe. Some have struggled to look for greener pastures in the diaspora. "When Zimbabwe's economy collapsed, most people fled for places such as South Africa, United Kingdom, and United States. Families were torn apart, and marriages never coped with the long distance."[10]

In a search on how Zimbabwean marriages are doing in the diaspora, I found a lament from a Zimbabwean woman in the diaspora. She and her friends were discussing the sad state of Zimbabwean marriages in the diaspora. Each conversation led her to think of a conversation with another Zimbabwean, which said nothing good about Zimbabwean marriages in the diaspora. This was not because they chose to,

---

[10]   *newsdzezimbabwe.co.uk/2012/01/divorce-in-zim-blame-diaspora-says-high.html.*

but simply because the divorce rate among Zimbabweans has reached unbelievable heights. For two months, she pondered and lamented. She realized she could not come up with a single reason as to why the divorce rate among Zimbabweans in the diaspora was increasing year in and year out.

In her lamentation, she wonders if the problem is due to the pressure to make things work out well for the families in Zimbabwe and in the diaspora. She says it could be that Zimbabweans in the diaspora easily give up; they have become too impatient and are unrealistic about life situations in the diaspora. She wonders if things are the way they are because Zimbabweans in the diaspora have become too materialistic, blindly adopting the Western culture without first gaining a better understanding of it. She argues that most of the issues dividing Zimbabwean families in the diaspora would have had no effects on those families if they were living in Zimbabwe. They would resolve the issues amicably in order to look good and mature in the eyes of family members and friends in Zimbabwe.

*   *   *

Zimbabwean Gets Life for Killing Wife in UK

In one of the Zimbabwean websites I visited, I found a report by Suzy Gibson of a Zimbabwean man, still struggling to have asylum status granted him in the United Kingdom, who brutally stabbed his wife five times while she was asleep. The reason for stabbing his wife was that she had an affair with his half-brother the night before. The woman, woken from her sleep by the stabbing to her chest and back, staggered into the hallway in a struggle to save her life. She fell and died there last August 31. To the surprise of everyone, the man denied the murder charges, arguing that his wife provoked him and that he acted in self-defense.[11] How a sleeping woman attacked him, I do not understand. The thirty-five-year-old asylum seeker, who suddenly became an animal because of his wife's extramarital affair, was found guilty of murdering the mother of his three beautiful daughters.

Another Zimbabwean, this time in the United States, is reported to have beaten life out of his girlfriend and then burning her remains to cover up the crime. The road that led to the death and burning of this woman started over a bitter argument about dirty dishes left in the sink. During the argument, the girl hit her boyfriend with her

---

[11]   www.newzimbabwe.com/pages/uk2.11871.html.

purse. In anger, he turned around and beat his girlfriend to death. After realizing he had squeezed life out of his girlfriend, he dragged her lifeless body into the garage and burned it, not because it is expensive to bury people in the Western world, but because he wanted to cover up his crime. Maybe he did not know brutal actions like his can hardly escape the watchful eyes of the Western government and police.

The late woman's eight-year-son told the police that from his room he heard his mother crying for help, but he thought that it was a dream. The man told the police he was unable to recall the details of all that took place before the woman died. Because the man had no criminal history, he was not charged with a crime that would bring life imprisonment or the death penalty. He only faces twenty-two to twenty-seven years imprisonment, with the chance of parole after he has served about thirteen years in prison. His passport was confiscated, so he may not run away after the payment of $1 million in bail.[12]

---

[12]   *http://zimbabweonlinepress.com/index.php?news=3861.*

Nigerian Marriages in the Diaspora

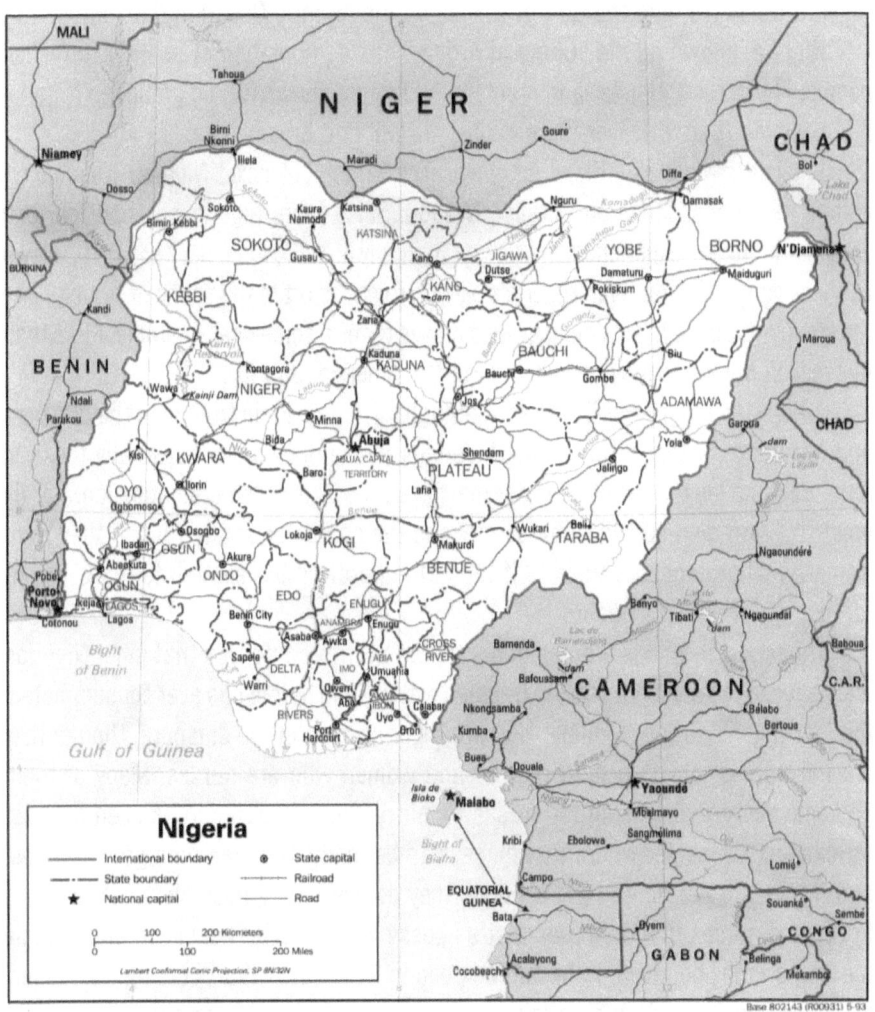

Pray for Nigeria, pray for Africa

The Federal Republic of Nigeria has thirty-six states. The capital at Abuja. Nigeria covers a surface area of about 356,000 square kilometers, making it the thirty-second—largest country on earth. European leaders in Bismarck's "bedroom" decided Nigeria's boundaries without any African's knowledge. Nigeria shares boundaries with the Republic of Benin in the west, Cameroon and Chad in the east, Niger in the north, and the Gulf of Guinea on the Atlantic Ocean in the south.

Nigeria, known as the "China of Africa," has a population of about 120 million people. The Yoruba, Hausa, and Igbo are the largest known ethnic groups in Nigeria. It is believed that wherever there is life, you will find Igbo people.

English is Nigeria's official language. The British colonized Nigeria. The country gained its independence on October 1, 1960. Since then, Nigeria has had fourteen presidents. Nigeria experienced a civil war from July 6, 1967, to January 15, 1970, known as the Nigerian-Biafran War. Nigeria's oil-rich region is often the scene of trouble, and the steady rise of radical Islamic groups makes Nigeria somewhat unstable. More than five million Nigerians may be living in Europe, America, and Asia.

A Nigerian reporter writes that Nigerian marriages are in trouble in the diaspora and the main reason is that many Nigerians in the diaspora—especially those in America—no longer see or consider marriage as a God-ordained institution. Nor do most Nigerian men consider the beauty and the character of any woman they want to marry. What concerns them is if the girl is hardworking enough to make money for him and if she has papers.

The reporter, who is a nurse in the United States, confesses that most Nigerian marriages in the diaspora start in troubled waters, and before it is ever consummated, the marriage is already sinking. He says Nigerian men in the diaspora, though they are not nurses, are in a mad rush to find women who are nurses. Many of them go home every year looking for nurses to marry. Since health care is seen by most Africans as the sector where fast money can be made, Nigerian men go for nurses, and if they are not able to get a nurse, they do everything possible for their wives to become nurses in America as fast as possible. No matter how good and humble the woman may be, even if she can be good in fields other than nursing, her dollar-hungry husband sees her as a failure and a disappointment. She has to be a nurse in order to make money for her husband.

Another reason Nigerians marriages easily break up in the United States concerns the woman's green card or resident permit. Single Nigerian women in America with papers are goddesses. Some may not be nurses, but undocumented Nigerian men scramble for them. Whoever gets her treats her with tender care and religious respect. But the moment he gets his own papers through his wife, he walks away to search for a nurse, who will make money for him. Let it be clear this is not the character of all Nigerians in the diaspora.[13]

Another Nigerian website states that even ants are aware that most Nigerian marriages are in trouble in America and no longer worthy to be called marriages. Some are hanging on a tiny rope, which can be cut off at any moment. Others marriages are already in a state of separation or ended by divorce. Nigerian marriages in the diaspora are also subject to brutality. Any little domestic dispute suddenly becomes brutal. In some cases, the marriage has a deadly end.

*   *   *

One of the deadly cases I found took place in Grand Praise, Texas. It is reported that a forty-six-year-old Nigerian woman was forced to join her ancestors by her husband on September 8, 2005, just a day after her birthday. With tears and regret, the deceased's uncle told news reporters how nice his late niece was. With uncontrolled anger, her husband drove for about thirteen hours just to kill his wife. The uncle also said that the late woman's marriage was in constant trouble, but because of shame and the thought she would not be able to bear the stigma her community would place on her if she called the police about her husband's threats, she never called the police. Still in tears, he confessed that he shared the blame of not reporting the matter to the police when the sun was still shining, since he had a good knowledge of what was going on.[14]

*   *   *

In Washington DC, a thirty-six-year-old Nigerian registered nurse was stabbed to death with a kitchen knife by her forty-one-year-old husband from Abia. The woman had received news of the death of her father in Nigerian. Her desire to go to Nigeria and give her late father a befitting burial was angrily opposed by her husband, arguing there were many bills to be paid. Since she was the one earning a living, she left for Nigeria against the will of her husband. On her return from her three-week

---

[13]   www.naijapals.com/modules/naijapals/dis-life!/the-untold-truth-about-american-marriages-(nigerians-in-diaspora).

[14]   www.kwenu.com/publications/orabuchi/nigerian_marriages.htm.

stay in Nigeria and the satisfactory burial of her beloved father, she was murdered by her dollar-hungry husband. He was charged with first-degree murder of his wife.[15]

*　*　*

Another Nigerian registered nurse, this time in Tennessee, was gunned down together with her mother by her husband. Like other many Nigerian men, he married this intelligent girl in Nigeria and brought her to America. In America, he sent her to nursing school. Upon her graduation and qualification as a registered nurse, reporters found the man could not recognize his wife any more; it was as though she had become another person. Repeatedly, this woman called police against her husband and some of his nights were spent in the jail cell. It did not end just there; he lost his house to his wife. He also lost custody of his children and could only see them periodically. She made it very hard for him to see the children at the court-scheduled time.

He was given a death sentence for killing his wife and his mother-in-law.[16]

*　*　*

In Garland, Texas, another registered nurse of Nigerian origin, was murdered by her husband, this time on March 25, 2007.

Close family and friends told reporters the mother of the late registered nurse was found dead not two years later, while visiting from Nigeria. She was found dead in a bathtub in the same house where her daughter was found dead—mysteriously, like her mother. The nurse's husband used a hammer to beat her into her grave when was deep asleep. People wondered if he had also murdered the visiting mother-in-law. The wife killer was sentenced to life in prison without parole. [17]

African Marriages as Business Ventures

In the Nigerian communities in the diaspora, marriage is viewed as a business. In these communities, black clouds of trouble and uncertainty cover each family as they struggle to find their feet in the Western culture, so different from that of their homeland. They struggle to make it together with their children in their new country

---

[15]　*www.meniru.blogspot.com/2008/06/nigerian-men-wife-killers.html.*
[16]　*www.meniru.blogspot.com/2008/06/nigerian-men-wife-killers.html.*
[17]　*www.republicreport.com/dubem-okafor-another-nigerian-man-kills-his-wife-in-the-usa-written-by-icheoku.*

as well as extended family back in Nigeria. African men and women carry around unending complains about each other in the diaspora. Women complain that

- African men do not give them flowers.
- African men do not know how to work with women to make better decisions.
- African men in the diaspora suffer from an inferiority complex.
- African men are afraid of African women, who are earning more money than they are.
- African men in the diaspora may be too slow in their growing process.

African men have the following to say about African women in the diaspora.

- African women in the diaspora are wayward.
- African women in the diaspora are very ungrateful.
- They are self-centered and greedy in every aspect of their lives.
- They are never willing to cooperate with men.
- African women are unpredictable. You never know what they want from men and how they want to be treated by African men. In the morning, she wants to be treated like an African woman; at noontime, she wants to be treated in a way she has just invented; and in the evening, she wants to be treated like a Western woman.

Because of this confusion and accusations, African men and women search for comfort and acceptance in different places. In this struggle, men have a greater advantage than women. They are able to move on with life and marry wherever and whenever they want. That is why many Nigerian men are marrying white women, and many return to Nigeria to marry any woman they want. The women they go for in Africa are believed not to have been brainwashed by the Western worldview. Their views on marriage are formed by the African culture or by their religious beliefs. They are satisfied with a life centered on the family and her husband.

Not so with the Nigerian woman in the diaspora. It is very difficult for an educated Nigerian woman to go to Nigeria and marry a man who is not as educated as she is. Women would love to marry men who are more educated than they. Their pride keeps them from marrying less-educated men; men do not have that problem when it comes to less-educated women.

It is easily said all Nigerians do about marriage is wrong. They marry the wrong person for the wrong reasons and at wrong times. Many do not know what marriage is all about. They do not know that a healthy marriage is the fruit of hard labor and selfless sacrifice. Because of the lack of knowledge about what it takes to be married, their marriages in the diaspora often end in divorce. When things are not working, some seek help from the spiritual realm, like witch doctors, medicine men, or voodoo. Some men who have labored financially and had walked through US laws to bring their wives to America find it very hard to forgive them when the women leave them just when their husbands need them the most. Life for the woman leaving her husband in the diaspora in the quest for independence and a better life finds it more difficult if she has children from that relationship.

Nigerian men and women are called on to reconsider their concept of marriage. They are told not to rush into marriage and that marriage should never be looked at as a means to help one out of poverty.[18]

---

[18]   *www.africanexecutive.com/modules/magazine/articles.php?article=1081.*

Ghanaian Troubled Marriages in the Diaspora

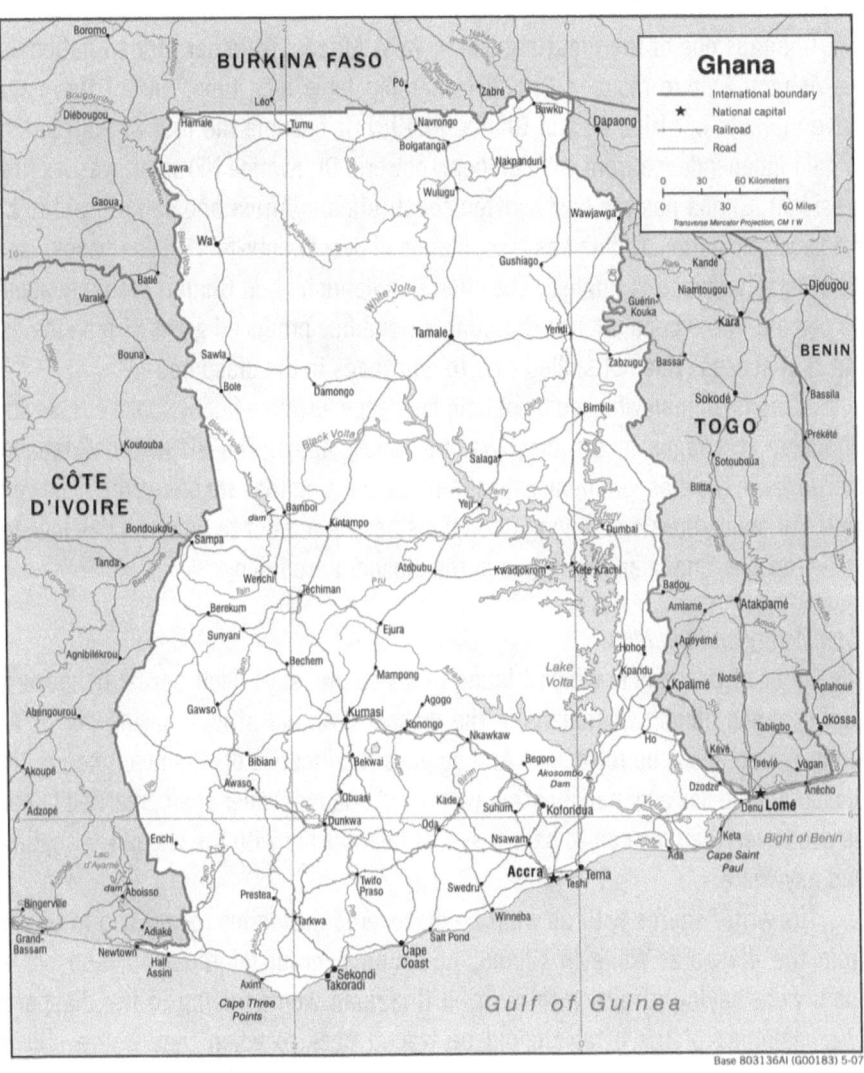

Pray for Ghana, pray for Africa

First known as the Gold Coast, the country changed its name to Ghana after its independence. Dr. Kwame Nkrumah, in his independence speech, first mentioned the new name. Some say the name came from the then-Ghana Empire, stretching from Sudan to Mali. Lovers of Dr. Nkrumah say Ghana means "God has appointed Nkrumah already for Africa."

Ghana is one of the great nations in West Africa. Like other African nationals, the Ashanti Empire resisted British leadership for a long time. One of the major slave markets in Africa was in Ghana. In 1957, it became the first African nation to gain independence from the European powers. Dr. Kwame Nkrumah was its first president. Ghana has the best-written constitution in Africa and can be said to be a democratic nation. Ghana has a population of over twenty-four million people, and its official language is English. The church is flourishing in Ghana; probably about 75 percent of the population is Christian. Ghana has produced great African minds. But that success has not spilled over to marriages in the diaspora.

A Ghanaian man who could not hold his peace anymore finally spoke out, saying Ghanaian marriages in the diaspora are falling apart. The attack on Ghanaian marriages in the diaspora demolishes families, causing the rate of divorce to be very high. For some, marriage among Ghanaians has turned out to be deadly. Below are some reasons Ghanaian marriages in the diaspora are failing.

Promiscuity and Infidelity
The writer of this article which I found in a website, says illicit sexual behavior is very common among Ghanaians in the diaspora. An old African saying goes, "An old path can easily be retraced." And so goes the lifestyle of Ghanaian men in the diaspora. If he has ever had an affair with a girl and meets her again, married or not, he does everything he can to have a sexual relationship with the woman—anytime and anywhere.

The writer shares with us what he discovered during his recent trip to Ghana from the diaspora. While in Ghana, he found a group of ten men, and six of them were having affairs with married Ghanaian women living in the diaspora. The beginning of the affairs could be traced back to when they where still in high school. He knew all the women, and surprising to him, all are committed Christians in their Ghanaian churches in the diaspora. He confessed that one of these unfaithful women sent him with a parcel to give her boyfriend in Ghana, telling the writer that the man is her brother. On delivering the parcel, he found out the man was, in truth, her boyfriend. He recalled seeing the woman with her husband at a funeral service in the United States. He wished the husband knew what he discovered.

One may begin to think that only Ghanaian women are caught in these dirty affairs, but Ghanaian men in the diaspora are worse. They have secret, extramarital affairs in Ghana and wherever they are living. Like the women, they send large sums of money to their secret lovers in Ghana.

The writer is an insider in the Ghanaian community in the diaspora and knows almost all the nasty things happening in the community. He says marital unfaithfulness is the cause of the high rate of HIV/AIDS among Ghanaian couples everywhere. He talks of a married Ghanaian woman who worked as a live-in nurse, not knowing the very rich patient she was taking care of was HIV positive. Her hunger for money caused her to give herself to the man in exchange for money. The man did not only give her money; he also gave her HIV/AIDS. The money she received was not enough to take care of her HIV, and she also infected her innocent husband with the disease. This took place in New York.

In another trip to Ghana, he discovered a well-known lawyer who died of AIDS in Ghana was having an affair with a married Ghanaian woman in the diaspora. When she heard that her boyfriend died of AIDS, she rushed for the HIV/AIDS test, and the results were positive. She lied to her friends, telling them she got it through a contaminated blood transfusion, but deep down in her heart, she knows the truth. And God knows it, too.

The Ghanaian community in the diaspora serves as a good facilitator of extramarital affairs. The leaders of the little groups in the community use their positions to prey on married women and some young girls. Each passing day, married Ghanaian men are caught red-handed in extramarital affairs. Even the clergy are not immune to such affairs. In Canada, one clergyman suffered a heart attack during an act of unfaithfulness with his girlfriend and died.

Churches
Ghanaian churches in the diaspora are blamed for not offering a solution to the mess. Instead, they have become advocates and contributors to the causes of divorce among Ghanaians in the diaspora. Ghanaian men with no divine call on their lives to the pastoral ministry are filling pulpits with lots of false prophesies. They pull married women out of the arms of their husbands every week.

These churches are loaded with lots of programs. About four days a week, the man will not see his wife, who is spending all her free time in the church for choir

21

practice, Bible study, women's group meetings, and unnecessarily long Sunday worship services. It is worse when the husband attends a different church, where worship lasts no longer than an hour. He goes home, and his wife returns from her church about five hours later, because according to her, the Holy Spirit moved their pastor to keep on preaching. But it is not the Holy Spirit; it is poor time management.

Once she's at home, the woman keeps talking on the phone with one friend after another. Staying on the phone and the Internet for hours may be a sign the marriage is giving way, and that your spouse's heart is no longer in the marriage. Every week she fasts, and during her fasting, she is not to have sex with her husband, a decision made in disobedience of 1 Corinthians 7:4-7.

> The wife does not have authority over her own body but yields it to her husband. In the same way, the husband does not have authority over his own body but yields it to his wife. Do not deprive each other except perhaps by mutual consent and for a time, so that you may devote yourselves to prayer. Then come together again so that Satan will not tempt you because of your lack of self-control. I say this as a concession, not as a command. I wish that all of you were as I am. But each of you has your own gift from God; one has this gift, another has that.

Money

It is not surprising to hear that money is one of the causes of divorce among Ghanaians in the diaspora. Ghanaians in the diaspora glory in having building projects back in Ghana. The sorrowful part of it is that spouses do not know about most of these projects.

The family becomes a battleground when the husband accidentally discovers his wife is secretly sending money for a project he knows nothing about, or when the wife discovers her husband is sponsoring a project in Ghana without her knowledge. Those who manage the projects in Ghana are their secret boyfriends and girlfriends, who end up using the money to fund their personal projects. When the innocent partner in the diaspora goes to Ghana to inspect the work, he or she finds out it was a ghost project back home.

My Story

The writer of this article is not a stranger to all he is writing about. It happened to him, but he was too blind to see his wife had divorced him in her soul long ago. His eyes were opened when it was already too late. He and his wife were sleeping in different bedrooms, and they hardly made love. If they did, it was two times a month, after a long struggle. His stay-at-home wife, who was a committed member of their Ghanaian church in the diaspora, was always tired. She would do everything to go to Ghana as often as possible. Even if it were not possible, she would force him to make it possible. He eventually learned she was continuing her affair with her secondary—school boyfriend. That was why she always seemed to be on her way to Ghana; she was going to have fun with her boyfriend.

The couple divorced and went their separate ways. His ex-wife continued her affair with her secondary-school lover, who promised her heaven on earth. These were promises only a foolish woman would accept, promises never to be fulfilled. Even though the boyfriend was married, his ex-wife was still dying for him, and bought air tickets for him to visit her in America before and after their divorce. She used the money she got from their divorce settlement to buy cars for her boyfriend in Ghana.

Not long afterward, she had a stroke and was flown to Ghana. You would think the boyfriend she adored would come to her aid, but he never visited her or helped her. It was I—her divorced husband, the father of her three children—who helped her until her painful death in Ghana. She had squandered all her money by wild living, and the boyfriend was gone with the cars.

Open Challenge to Pastors

The writer wants all Ghanaian pastors—all African pastors in the diaspora—to read this article to their congregations and ask those who are guilty of any of the issues he has presented as causes of the high rate of divorce in the diaspora to confess. He wants the church to help in healing the trouble family, not become a divider of families, as many African churches in the diaspora have become.[19]

---

[19]   *www.ghanaweb.com/GhanaHomePage/diaspora/artikel.php?ID=108011.*

Ethiopian Troubled Marriages in the Diaspora

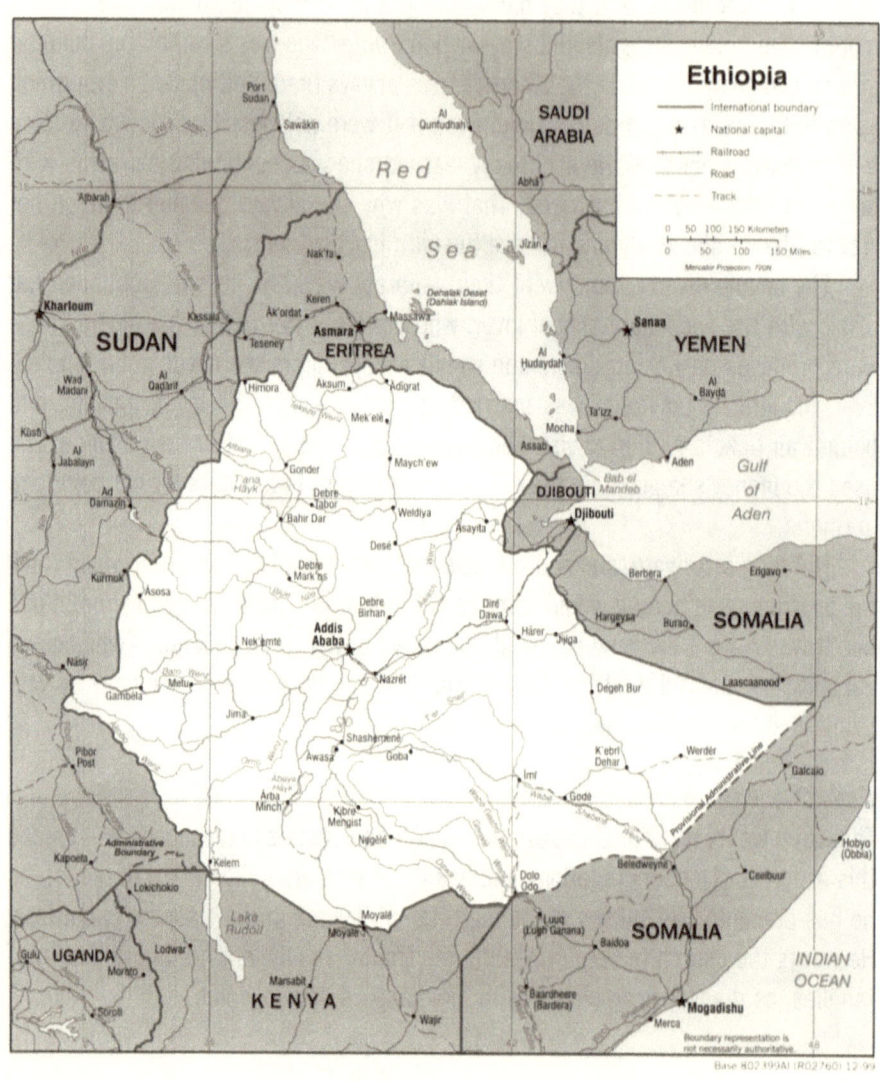

Pray for Ethiopia, pray for Africa

Ethiopia was formally known as Abyssinia. Scholars say Abyssinia means "mix," while the word "Ethiopia" is from Greek words for "burn" and "face." This may be a description of the people living in this land; the people of this land might have been of mixed race.

Ethiopia, one of the oldest nations under the sun, is the only African nation European powers never colonized. It is one of the African nations mentioned in the Bible. We know of the Ethiopian eunuch, and it is said that the Queen of Sheba who visited King Solomon came from Ethiopia. Some who do not believe the Bible creation account hold that human life started in Ethiopia. Some consider one of the leaders of Ethiopia, Emperor Haile Selassie, to be a messiah. The gates of hell have greatly attacked the church in Ethiopia, but with all the troubles, the Ethiopian church marches on, just like in the days of Pentecost.

Many Ethiopians are leaving their nation and settling in the diaspora. Their marriages in the diaspora are also in trouble.

*   *   *

One of the Internet sites used to research this topic reports that a nineteen-year-old woman, a Norwegian citizen of Ethiopian origin, was found dead in Norway. Her body was found in an apartment in the Anker Studentbolig complex in Oslo, near the Anker River. The victim's husband, also of Ethiopian origin, was nowhere to be found. Because of blood found at the scene, police concluded the young girl was murdered, and the person of interest was her twenty-seven-year-old husband, who had disappeared.

The woman left Ethiopia for Norway in 2000, and in 2006, she was granted Norwegian citizenship. The missing husband came to Norway on an F1 visa, and in 2006, they got married. She was murdered just as they were about to celebrate their second anniversary. Norwegian police issued warrants for his arrest.[20]

*   *   *

An Ethiopian woman, this time in the state of Virginia in the United States, died in the hospital after all attempts by skillful and merciful medical doctors had failed. She was suspected to have been choked or suffocated by her Ethiopian husband, who was already in the net of Arlington, Virginia, police. The deceased Ethiopian

---

[20]   www.ethiopianreview.com/content/2816.

was her husband's forerunner to America. When she came to the United States, she did her very best so her husband and their three-year-old son could join her in America. She labored tirelessly as a server in an Arlington restaurant. She used her hard earned dollars to bring her husband to America. He showed his gratitude by choking her to death.[21]

*　　*　　*

Ethiopian Man Kills Mother, Daughter in Virginia

About 10:30 a.m., police in Alexandria received a call from an apartment around 375 South Reynolds Street, asking them to rush to what the caller said was a domestic disturbance. The police arrived at the scene, on the fourteenth floor, and found a beautiful, lifeless, Ethiopian woman and her three-year-old daughter believed to have been murdered by her husband and father, who had disappeared. The Alexandria police are doing everything to smoke him out of his hiding place to face charges of first-degree murder. Even though they were only cohabiting, her killer did not have the right to murder her and her innocent daughter.[22]

---

[21]　*Ibid.*
[22]　*Ibid.*

Cameroonian Troubled Marriages in the Diaspora

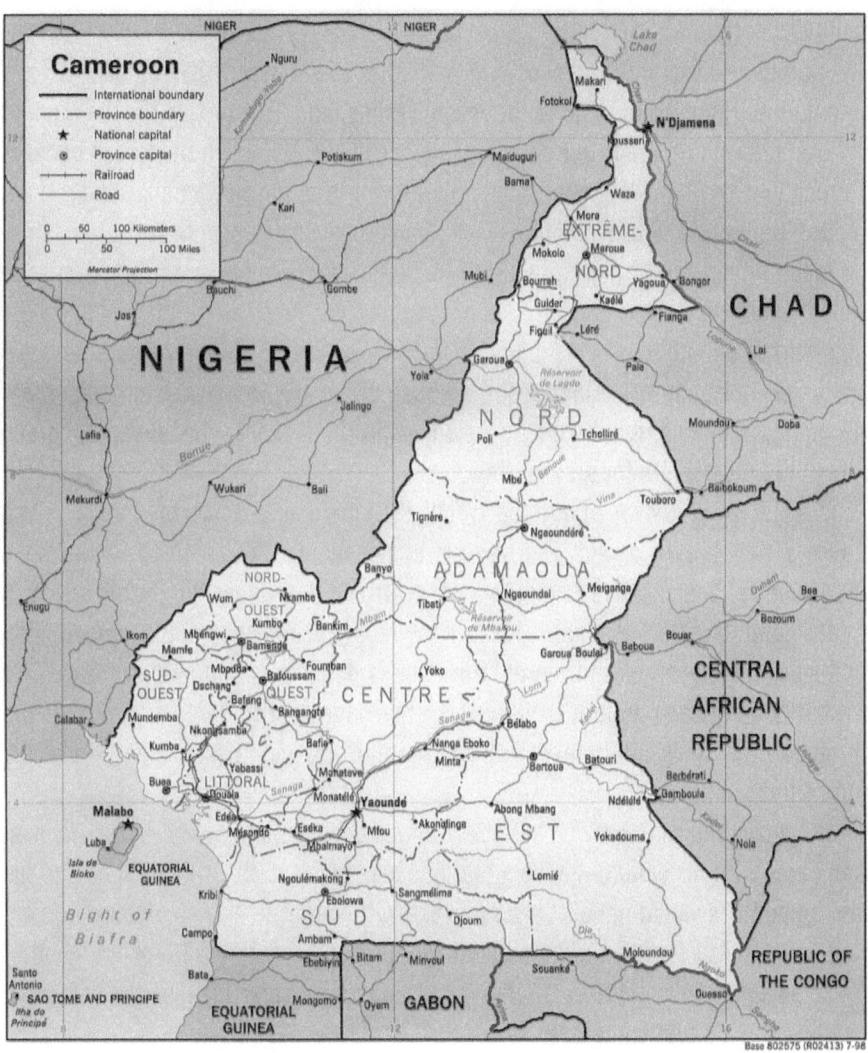

Pray for Cameroon, pray Africa

Cameroon is the only bilingual nation in Africa, with English and French as its official languages, though all official documents are written in French. It is okay to say Cameroon is in Central Africa or West Africa due its geographic position. French-speaking Cameroonians in the East would say that Cameroon is in Central Africa; English-speaking Cameroonians west of the Mongo River would say that Cameroon is in West Africa.

Cameroon was a German colony, and after World War I, it was seized from defeated Germany and shared between France and Britain by the League of Nations. French Cameroon got its independence in 1960; English Cameroon became independent the following year by simply leaving Nigeria and joining its brothers in East Cameroon. Since independence, Cameroon has had only two presidents. Ahmadou Ahidjo was the first. In 1982, he handpicked Paul Biya as his successor. He is the current leader.

As rich as Cameroon is, many of its people live in poverty. It seems as if corruption is legalized in Cameroon. Because of poverty, many Cameroonians are leaving their homeland in search of new lives in the diaspora, because the "green grass" in Cameroon is for a select few.

Very little is known about the troubles Cameroonian marriages face in the diaspora Well known or not, the story is somehow identical with those we have already read. The disease affecting many African marriages in the diaspora is spreading among Cameroonians, leaving the hearts of many men and women filled with sorrow, bitterness, and regret. The virus is dangerous and has no respect for any marriage. It has painfully destroyed the marriages of the clergy and laities from Cameroonians living in England, France, Spain, Germany, Russia, China, America, and so forth.

A Cameroonian couple wed in December and divorced in January. A Cameroonian man came with his wife to the diaspora. Because of the issue of papers, he and his wife agreed she would have a fake marriage with someone else to procure a green card for her. Sad to say, the agreement the husband thought was for the good of the struggling family in the diaspora was an end to their marriage, as the wife went for papers and never came back.

Another Cameroonian woman in the diaspora labored so hard, working three jobs, saving money, and sleeping in her car to bring her husband to the white man's land. She paid for her husband to join her in the diaspora and rented an apartment for the family when he was on his way to America.

When the husband arrived, he saw many white girls and said to himself, *Since my mama born me, I have never tested a white girl.* He abandoned his wife, saying that, if she were beautiful, she would not have struggled to bring him to the white man's land. She would have found a white man to marry her.

Marital unfaithfulness among Cameroonians in the diaspora is so high that some are picking up guns and going to jail.

*   *   *

A Cameroonian man living in Columbus, Ohio, finally admitted to have shot dead his wife's suspected boyfriend a little more than four years after the crime was committed. In December 2005, the Cameroonian man is said to have seen his wife leave a hotel room with another Cameroonian, whom he believed his wife was having an extramarital affair with. They got into her car, the woman driving and her boyfriend in the passenger seat. Her husband followed them and shot the man in the back on Interstate 185 North, between Macon Road and the Manchester Expressway. In court, he pleaded guilty of the crime during a struggle to get lesser charges.

It is said the man bought the gun the same day he shot his wife's secret boyfriend. As many Cameroonians have never fought a war, and guns are not part of their lives, he pleaded with someone to teach him how to load it. The gunman's lawyer said his client is a nice man. It was the news of his wife's affair that led him to act the way he did. He was sentenced to twenty-five years. He could apply for parole after twelve years.

The Voices of Single African Ladies in the Diaspora
I found this wonderful article written by concerned single African women in the diaspora. It does not talk about marriages breaking up, but it presents the difficulties faced by single African women in the diaspora who are waiting for African men to ask them for marriage, but none are coming. Reading it helps one to know the minds of single African women.

> To: African Men in the Diaspora
> From: African Women in the Diaspora
> Re: Several Issues We Wish to Discuss! Plus, You Are Our Only Hope
> July 24, 2009
>> What I want to say is so important, and I do not want anything to stand in the way of what I want to say. I am trying to write in

a language all of us will understand. I do not care about correct tenses and punctuations for they will slow me down.

We the single African women in the diaspora met together and decided that it was time for us to take some things off our shoulders. Even though our light-skin sisters refuse to share in our concern, we know that they are going through what we are going through, day in and day out.

Mansa, an attractive and educated African lady in the diaspora just got information from Ghana that her twenty-five-year-old little sister got married. Even though she was happy for her baby sister, she was also very jealous because she was almost forty and has not been fortunate enough to be married. Mansa wasn't the only one panicing; we, her single sisters in the diaspora, are joining her in her uneasiness. We, the single African women in the diaspora, have realized that if we do not ask serious questions about our marital lives, we will soon die old and lonely in our nice homes with our big degrees and fancy cars. Because of this concern, we come to you, our African men in the diaspora, to ask you where we went wrong. We want to know—from you—why you do not want to marry us. You are marrying other races while we are slowly fading away. If you keep doing this to us, we shall all die out leaving no seeds and no traces of our human existence. We African single women in the diaspora are fast becoming one of Africa's endangered species, and we want to know why you treat us with little or no concern.

We are confused. White men don't want us, to them we black women are not beautiful. Our black men are afraid to marry us, saying that we are too educated and not willing to be submissive. We have found ourselves wanting in the diaspora, as European men will only get married within their circle. Asian men are the worst for all they think is that we have to sponsor their business as we stream to their stores all day buying different things. We have resolved to weaves and creams. It has become very difficult for us to be ourselves.

Our sister Amma met with another sister of ours from Kenya a few days ago. She looked terrible. She was what some call "coke and fanta." Her face was light having the color of fanta while her neck was darker—the color of coke. This reveals her struggles to look attractive.

Another Nigerian sister has gone to the point where we do not know what she is doing with her hair. Cecilia says she met her and almost passed by without knowing who she was because she changes her styles every day.

I come from Ghana. I do not want to start talking about my Ghanain sisters because I know them so well and I do not want to embarrass any of them. Some Ghanain women even want to change the color of their eyes. In addition, when they talk, you will hear the heavy African accent, yet they struggle to talk with a Western accent just to see if they can attract a man.

While we were still in our different nations in Africa, you ran behind us saying how you would die for us. Even the height of the fences around our compounds, complete with barbed wire and the dangerous broken bottles made it impossible for anyone to jump over, could not stop you. Your love for us gave you the skills of a cat with which you were always jumping over the fences unhurt. Even when our parents threatened to gun you down or call the police, you still could not stop calling. With all the beautiful natural flowers around and in poverty, you chose to buy us artificial flowers.Even though we accepted them; it was just because we knew how you had struggled to put money together for months in order to afford that for us. I still have a good memory of a teddy bear bought for me as a Valentine's gift, which I gladly named Kwame Snuggly. I still love and highly esteem Kwame, who gave me the teddy bear, and I dream of him each night whenever I recall the sacrifices he made for our love and for the joy we once shared. I can still hear his voice telling me how I am his African queen. I remember how he used to sing of my beauty. Now in his cruelty in the diaspora all he says about me is opposite of all he said when we were still in Africa. This world and its people are terrible and wicked.

When we were becoming mature girls, our mothers in Africa told us that if we did not know how to cook and clean the compound, we would never have a good man to marry us. We accepted the challenge of cooking and cleaning together with the educational challenges. We did the cooking in our mother's kitchen; we went to the farm and cleaned the compound; we read and did our home work late at night. Yet you did not do better than we did though you had all the time on earth to play your football and do your homework. Having a wife who does not know how to cook is a disgrace to her husband and to her parents. One of our mothers said education is not good for girls; men will run away from highly educated girls. Sometimes now, I seem to think that she was right. Look at us, how many of us highly educated women are married? Even though we have humbled ourselves to the lowest level? We have done everything. We have even trimmed our hips, thighs, and buttocks. Yet you are still complaining. Now we want to be accepted and appreciated by African men just as we are. We do not want to heavily decorate ourselves anymore to be attractive.

The love and passion to make my husband happy compelled me to learn to do things that I personally hate. One of them is egusi stew. I thought I may marry a husband who loves egusi stew, and it would not be good for me, his wife, not to be able to cook it for him. Yet the men I had prepared myself for are choosing other women who can not cook what they like.

As our humble mothers in Africa trained us, we have not changed. We still know how to cook egusi stew, and yam and other things. We are well educated and able to do multiple jobs as we did at home. That is why many of us were able to navigate our way through two jobs and our university studies. Our education has helped us to be able to sustain a sound discussion with you and your friends without embarrassing you. We know almost everything other women know. We know how to serve people at home with wine. We know how to drink wine and eat those things the women you are running after are eating, though we would prefer our simple, healthy African food. We, your African women, know what moves an African man.

Emmanuel, one of my cousins says that he prefers akata girls to African girls. What pains me the most is that he was present and agreeing with my grandmother and auntie when they were saying that the fastest way to reach a man's heart is through his stomach. Now that I know all the cooking and am ready to use it to reach the heart of any African man, they all prefer akata girls who will want breakfast, lunch, and supper to be from a restaurant.

Now is the time for us to right all the wrongs. Blaming each other repeatedly will not help us in any way. African men, we want you to tell us what we, your beautiful African girls, have done for you to trash us for other women. Tell us any other thing but not that "falling in love" empty stuff. We also want to be loved, and we know how to show love to those who love us too. Give us real flowers and work your way into our hearts. Even when we love you and we want to make "girls" for the building of love stories and laughter for the future.

African men complain that we have changed since we came to the diaspora. We wander why changing to better ourselves is a problem for African men. Our learning is to enable us to support you with the bills and other immediate and extended family issues. Our change is all for you and the good of our family.

Our sister Abena believes that the reason African men are running away from us educated African women is because they think we have better degrees, better jobs, better cars, and are making better money, and African men feel that with this they cannot control us like house helps. We are very indepentant, free to visit you any time and ready to drive off whenever you start talking rubbish.

As for me, I strongly hold that African men are running from us because we know them so well, and they are running to women who do not know their background as we do. We know how you were when you were eleven years old. We know where you started. We saw you running around without shoes. We sat with you in school, and we know how you were struggling to catch up with us. Still we love to be your wives, why run away?

We have not understood where you are running to. We would love to have you come back to us. We will treat you better and love you deeply.

At the meat market a few weeks ago Akosua, one of our Africa sisters, met a Ghanaian man with his akata wife and their little child. Accidentally, the child wandered away as little kids will do. The akata wife did the unspeakable. In anger, she shouted at the man and pointed using the "F word" at him in a public market. The African man could not say a word. None of us, I say it again, no African woman will talk to her husband in a market place like this. I weep for my African men; I weep and ask myself, is this what our handsome men are leaving us and running after? Like Mary and Joseph, we run around looking for the baby together in love without blaming any body. I wander if our African men have gotten anything from all that myself and our other African sisters are saying. If we have communicated, then you are still within our reach. If we haven't, then you are gone, really gone, and we wish you the best wherever you may be.

We are pleading with our African men to talk with us so that we may know what you want us to change in order to get you back. Yet we want you to know that we will not sacrifice our dignity and pride as African women in order to accommodate your wild life.[23]

* * *

In my continuous search for what Africans are saying about their marriages in the diaspora, I found one of them had written an essay on what single, African, educated women are going through in the diaspora. I could not get hold of the essay, but another African had chosen to react on the essay, and I paraphrase her writing here.

- The writer wonders how many black women from African are having a serious relationship with an African man in hopes of taking the next step into marriage.

---

[23]   www.nigeriavillagesquare.com/articles/n-amma-twum-baah/to-african-men-in-the-diaspora.html.

- The shortage of black African men who are handsome, educated, and have good character is making African women in the diaspora to live as if they are in a little container with few men to scramble for. Because of this, single African women go for anyone who comes their way. It is not easy for African singles to see attractive, handsome, black men in the diaspora, because even those these beautiful African women would never consider for marriage are running away from them, preferring white women.

I am troubled. I may never have the right man of my dream. There is no way I can even think of dating an Asian or a man from the Middle East. The cultures are far apart, and it may take a lifetime to adapt if one morning it happens I am married to a man from Asia. The fact that our parents may never accept our partners from these regions makes the option unnecessary.

However, human perfection is nothing but an illusion; single African women in the diaspora spend all their time looking for "Mister Perfect." Some blindly allow themselves to be controlled by their cultures. Since African culture has some unproductive and unacceptable aspects, there is no reason why people should play by its rules.

The attitude of some single African women in the diaspora is what has landed them in the circumstances in which they are languishing now. Most of them are just confused, not knowing whether they are African women in the diaspora or Western women unable to clearly state what they require of a man. Give these women a little chance, and most of them will want to sit on their husbands and ride them as horses, always threatening to call social services whenever he opens his mouth. No African man in his right mind—in Africa or in the diaspora—will approach a woman like this for whatever reason. Even if it is by mistake, he will consider it a fatal mistake.

A woman should not dream of having a man from Mars or Jupiter. What she should look for is one who is okay for her, not longing to marry a man with an impressive car or who lives in a home that is like a little heaven on earth. A man who lives as though he is the producer of American dollars. Women who spend their time looking for husbands to come to them from space come to their real selves very late in life, when all the good men have come by. But being prideful, they chased them away as unfit. Now they are complaining and begging for men, and none are coming. And one may never come. To the best of my knowledge, I know that most Nigerian men will marry women only from Nigeria. Ethiopian men will marry only Ethiopian women. And the same goes with other Africans in the diaspora.

African women in the diaspora who have reach the ceiling of education—I mean PhD holders, lawyers, and medical doctors—cry that African men in the diaspora prefer white women. Nevertheless, the truth is these white women are willing to work with African men, while most of the educated African women are just full of themselves. Their requirements have sent some chicken-hearted Africans in places like Houston, Chicago, New York, Philadelphia, and Los Angeles to almost rob banks and even sacrifice their souls to the Devil in their senseless struggles to meet the never-ending demands of their self-centered and greedy wives.

I have talked a lot about African women in the diaspora as if they are the only ones to be blamed. Many African men in the diaspora are satanic, crafty demons, and first-class liars gifted in the manipulation of women. They are deceitful destroyers of African women's future and marital dreams. They are good at using and then dumping one girl after the other. At the end, they go home in search of innocent and perhaps virginal girls to settle down with. However, I do not feel remorse for the African women Annie Brisibe-Porbeni mentioned in her essay. I do not know how a woman can be that outgoing, simple, respectful, friendly, and nice looking and not have men scramble over her for marriage as the Europeans scrambled for Africa. I wonder how many men they look down on and minimize for reasons they may not be willing to voice now.

It is not a secret that married people are highly honored in Africa, while unmarried men and women are voiceless. The women in the essay are those who have lived in the diaspora for more than five years. They are the ones seeking equality with men, something an African man may never accept. One thing these women should have known is that a woman is another woman's merciless enemy.

It is my humble opinion that in the twenty-first century, a woman, African or non-African, should not need a ring, a partner, or a man to be content in life. She does not need a man before having a child. My advice to African women in the diaspora is that they should stop allowing themselves to be tortured by what their community unconstructively says about them. African women should not sit and wait for others to cultivate their farms for them. They should hoe their own farms and plant what they would love to eat.[24]

---

[24]   www.africanexecutive.com/modules/magazine/articles.php?article=3989.

CHAPTER 2

Parasites in the Western Culture that Destroy Marriages

C ulture is the sum total of inherited beliefs and values that control the basic behavior of a community of people. All human behavior occurs within particular cultures and within socially defined contexts.[25] But in the West, many believe their culture is the best and should be exported to all the corners of the world, especially Africa. On the other hand, many Africans also hold that the Western culture is the best. All I know is that there is no divine human culture. No culture is superior to the other. All human cultures have their good and bad sides. The Western world that thinks it has the most enlightened culture is confused about marriage. In this so-called enlightened culture, ideas like faithfulness, trust, honor, and commitment in marriage are considered old and primitive. It often seems only when you are a public figure, such as a politician, does the community expect you to be faithful to your spouse. Many things in the Western culture contribute to the high rate of divorce.

Books, Magazines, Movies, and TV Shows
Many movies and TV shows in the Western world do not honor marriage. Killings and cheating spouses fill movies and television screens. Unmarried people kiss and go to bed with each other. Consciously or unconsciously, the people of this community have learned a lot from these books and television shows, and they are living what Hollywood has taught them. We see this in their married life. ABC's *Nightline* once

---

[25]   G. Sherwood Lingenfelter, *Ministering Cross-Culturally* (Grand Rapids, Mich.: Baker Books House, 2001), 18.

reported the rise of swingers' clubs and parties among young couples. The program also reported on the steady increase of divorce in the West, and suggested perhaps the swinging lifestyle contributed to the problem, even though organizers would disagree. Dr. Curtis Bergstrand, associate professor of sociology at Bellarmine University, and Jennifer Blevins Williams, also of the department of sociology at Bellarmine University, conducted a study about today's alternative marriage styles in the West. What follows is my paraphrasing of their report.

Some years ago, what we call today swinging was called wife swapping. No matter what it is called, the fact is that the concept is growing rapidly with all classes of people and more among married couples in the United States. Media houses in America are closely following the steady growth of swinging, trying to see if this lifestyle is doing anything good for American families. North American Swing Club Association reports they have branches in Canada, England, France, Japan, and Germany. These branches operate sophisticated swing clubs for all classes of swing couples.

What really is wife swapping, swinging, and an alternative lifestyle? It is the freedom within marriage to allow couples to have sex with as many people as possible, sometimes in the presence of the spouse. It is the acceptance of infidelity and the sharing of spouses free from jealousy. Swingers believe this alternative lifestyle fortifies their marital relationship sexually and otherwise. Since cheating has become very common among couples, swinging helps them to openly enjoy themselves sexually with whomever, without any accusations of or guilt about cheating. Instead of sneaking around to have sex, swingers prefer to do it openly and shamelessly. Swing clubs do have regulations, though one may think there is no code of ethics.

This alternative lifestyle needs to be studied, because it presents to the community another way of life—monogamy with open sexual relationships with other members of the club. It is fast becoming a major concern in the Western community. To a greater extent, wife swapping is the rejection of monogamy. Since couples are divorcing every day and children are abandoned to themselves, it will be good to examine this lifestyle if it will build families and keep husband and wife together for a long time. If the swinger's redefinition of marital love solves the problems of divorce and other social ills, it is worthy of society's appreciation.[26]

Swing life, alternative life, and wife swapping shows us the direction in which the Western world is going. They want human beings to become animals as a way of solving a moral problem. The Devil is at work, dehumanizing humankind, the crown of God's creation.

The following story is real. It took place at a Walmart in Kansas. A boy and girl, in the presence of other shoppers in the store, kissed and went on to have sex with little or no shame. In order to have their open-air, marketplace sex show, they stole from Walmart a tube of lubricant to help hasten their illicit action. The police arrested them.[27]

This shows us how morally decayed some humans have become. Western medication or solution for this may only worsen the situation. The Western concept of freedom is that which allows people to do what ever with their lives and believe whatever they like. It is freedom to sin and live in sin and boast about it. Swingers live a normal, daily life. An African woman or man may be working in the same office with them. Swingers find no problem with their lifestyle. They are good at sharing with friends the joy of living an alternative lifestyle, and they invite others to come and see. But they do not force anyone to come. Even if you go, you still have your freedom not to have sex, but you will watch them having sex with each other's spouse however they want. Seeing or hearing about this lifestyle as a viable option may mislead those with a weak mind or weak will. This is nothing but social madness. Believe it or not, the main problem is sin, and only Christ Jesus is the solution, be it in Africa or in the West.

Western Culture as a Disposable and Dumping Society
I looked around Los Angeles, where I have been for some time, and found it is very difficult to find someone to fix your shoes, your watch, or your television. Sometimes you can find computer maintenance shops. When you take your car to a garage, you can see when they say a part is bad, it is bad. The old one is removed, thrown away, and replaced with a new part. People do not try to fix things like we do in Africa.

---

26   *www.ejhs.org/volume3/swing/body.htm.*
27   *www.sowetanlive.co.za/news/world/2012/08/15/couple-have-sex-in-supermarket.*

Western culture is good at dumping anything that seems to give trouble. Why bother fixing it? We'll just get a new one.

This attitude has crept into Western marriages. Spouses do not have time to sit and fix any misunderstanding between them; at least they think they don't. One spouse dumps the other and moves on to get someone new, all with false expectations that it will be sweeter and better this time. When another problem comes up, they do just what they did with the previous marriage. In Western culture, some people live longer with their pets than with their spouse.

The Rights of Women/Feminism

Feminism in the Western culture has taken everything a woman can enjoy from a man. Men are without voices, without the ability to prove themselves as the family protectors. Because men know that whatever a woman says with tears is valid anywhere, they have decided to sit and watch them do the talking and whatever they want. No man wants to think of being a woman's hero, because feminists do not see whatever he does as an achievement.

Women have become self-sufficient in so many ways, partly out of necessity and partly out of frustration, because they often cannot depend on anyone other than themselves. Most men have abdicated being gallant, because they no longer feel needed. Amid their frustration at being robbed of what they think makes them men, their reaction is, "Fine. Do it yourself." Women are now running corporations and have become movers and shakers in the marketplace, but be careful. Do not sacrifice your femininity before you consider all it will cost you. A woman who behaves like a man will walk a lonely path, because she leads men to assume they are not needed.[28]

Lack of Extended Families

In Africa, when we talk of a family, we are not talking just about a husband, wife, and maybe two kids and a pet. To an African, a family is the strength of almost a whole village behind you. You do not belong to yourself but to the whole family. You do not live just for yourself but for the extended family. When problems come, they are those of the whole family. When a decision is to be made, he or she thinks of how deep the consequences will go. If it is a good decision, he or she goes for it with the

---

[28] Michelle McKinney Hammond, *How to Be Found by the Man You've Been Looking For* (Eugene, Ore.: Harvest House Publishers, 2005), 76-77.

extended family in mind. If it is a bad decision, he or she slows down and thinks of how it affects all of the family members.

Extended family relations help to keep marriages stable, as no one wants to be looked on as the bad one in the family, the one who could not keep his or her marriage intact. For the sake of the family, people do their best to keep their marriages together. This is missing in Western culture. The lack of it appears as weakness in families, as there is never a second thought about the effect an action will have on the extended family. No one steps in authoritatively to help. The court and the dollar-hungry lawyers, ready to prepare documents for divorce, give very little help.

Easy Path to Divorce

Broad and easy is the path of divorce in the Western world. "Easy" laws have been put in place, and anything can lead to divorce in the white man's land. These easy laws give power to the judges to terminate a marriage. It is widely believed the pain caused by a divorce is much less than the pain caused by the reason given for the split. People clearly do not terminate intimate relationships just because the law gives them the freedom to do so. Unhappily married people divorce because they seek happiness through new marital partners. The Law of Moses says a man must present a certificate of divorce to his wife to make it difficult for him to divorce her. It was not easy to obtain the certificate of divorce.

But in the West, lawyers make money by helping people get quick divorces. The assurance that family access will be shared after a divorce is called for more and more divorce cases. Because divorce laws favor women, any complaint she presents to a judge, mixed with some crocodile tears, immediately puts the man in the painful process of paying child support to the ex-wife. I have no problem with child support for some men are good at making children everywhere and running away from all that it takes in raising a baby. If I could follow the boys in my village (Kom) in Cameroon to take care of their out—of—wedlock—babies I will do so with wrath. If I could encourage all the girls in my village to make known the father of their out—of—wedlock baby so that they can sit up and face the challenges of child rearing I will do so. If I could stop parents in my village from writing their names in their grand-children's birth cirtificates as father of their daughters babies so that the real fathers of the babies be persuaded to take up their responsibilities, I will do. But the problem in the West is another extreme where some women prefer child support than building a happy family relationship where the child enjoys the presence of the father. Sometimes the man is sent out of his home and becomes homeless, while the ex-wife lives happily in what was once the family home. In some cases, the woman sells the house and enjoys the money with her new boyfriend. Some set fire to the home, which used to be like a little heaven, and burn it to ashes.

Western women are in love with this culture, and unfortunately, many African women in the diaspora are in a mad pursuit of it as well. Oh, God, help us. They struggle to get hold of anything negative about their partners that divorce lawyers can magnify to help them walk away richer from their marriages. Because no stigma is attached to divorce in the Western community, many people are getting divorced. Even though there is divorce in Africa, stigma goes along with it. In Africa, divorce weakens your position among your friends. People look at you as someone who could not handle his or her family. Sometimes your advice is not taken seriously. A divorced woman may end up with no serious friends, as parents will not want their daughters to make friends with a divorced woman. Husbands will not want their wives to be friends of a divorced woman. Because of the stigma of divorce, couples struggle to settle their differences, doing everything they can to avoid divorce and its shame. This is not the case in the West. No one cares how many times one has divorced. It is normal to divorce whenever you want. And so goes the saying, "Who cares? I don't care. It is my life." I also hear this on the lips of many African men and women. Too bad, Africans are not individualistic in their thinking. Even among Christians and pastors in the West, divorce is very common. Divorce to them is no longer something God hates. "I hate divorce says the Lord."

Acceptance of Cohabitation
The cohabitation rate in the West is very high. It seems to be an acceptable lifestyle. They cohabit, and the church stays silent to their immoral lifestyle. The availability of birth control makes it easy for people to cohabit for many years without having children. Some will have two to three children while only living together. When someone cohabits, there is freedom to move from one partner to the other. Studies have found that very few cohabitations endure. In one of our class discussions, we were told only 17 percent of cohabitations survive five years or more; only 7 percent last ten years or more. The General Household Survey has found those who cohabit before marriage are "60 percent more likely to have divorce after eight years of marriage."[29]

Marriage has always needed structural support through the law and public policy. This was so even when marriage rates were at their highest and divorce

---

[29] *Social Trends* 24 (1994), 38.

was strongly stigmatized. Some of the structural supports for marriage no longer exist. Social conventions and public attitudes have also changed. There is now very little stigma attached to living together before marriage. In the United States, heterosexual, nonmarital cohabitation has been mostly a transitional rather than long-term phenomenon, with most couples either marrying or breaking up within a few years. In some European countries, however, the shift from married to unmarried cohabitation has gone much further, with more couples in long-term relationships remaining unmarried.[30]

Remarriage Phenomenon

The divorce rate is high in the West because of remarriage. At one church, everywhere around me I heard men and women talking about their ex-spouses. A friend told me when his father divorced his fifth wife, he thought the old man had learned his lesson and would not marry again. To his greatest surprise, his father married his sixth wife. In the West, it seems as if a person's eyes are always looking for another who might look better. The moment a person gets hold of one, he or she leaves. It is a surprise among many Westerners to hear someone has been married to the same person for more than twenty years. Remarrying repeatedly makes the Western culture look childish to us Africans, yet they find no problem with it.

Westerners may see an African man who is a polygamist, one man married to two or three wives at the same time. When a Western man says he has six children from three women he was married to at different times, he forgets the African polygamist can also say he has six children from three women.

Marrying someone who comes to you with his or her children from a previous marriage is often a step toward another divorce. "Another common conflict that is usually ignored in marriage preparation arises when one or both partners have children from previous marriages. When you bring children into a marriage, it changes the dynamic from the start."[31]

---

[30]   William, Arland, Tharnton G. Axim, and Yu Xie, *Marriage and Cohabitation* (Chicago: The University Chicago Press, 1007), 76-80.
[31]   L. Robin Smith, *Lies at the Altar* (New York: Hyperion, 2006), 76.

CHAPTER 3

Laying a Better Foundation for a Durable Marriage

To help rescue African marriages in the diaspora, Africans in the diaspora need to build their marriages on a solid foundation. Many definitions are available for the word "foundation." In the context of this book, it means "reason," "purpose," "genesis," or "beginning." I will use foundation as the reason or purpose for which a person got married. How your relationship with a person started is very important. How you met each other will always be the foundation of your marriage and will play a negative or positive part in your marital life. Many African marriages in the diaspora are in trouble because of weak foundations.

People marry for lots of reasons—and not always good ones. Many marriages fail because the couple does not understand the purpose or principles of a successful marriage. Modern society's confusion about marriage leads to couples marrying for reasons insufficient to sustaining a healthy, lifelong relationship.[32]

If African marriages in the diaspora are to be rescued, the foundation of marriage must be reconsidered. Those still to marry will have to look for a better foundation for their marriages. I have presented the following as weak foundations, or reasons to be avoided, and better foundations to build your marriage upon.

---

[32] Munroe, 35.

Weak Marital Foundations

I Love Her Breasts

You need to sit with men to hear how they describe parts of a woman's body, like her legs, breasts, buttocks, and eyes, and how she walks and talks. Many women know this very well. That is why they have resorted to dressing half naked. If you go to African parties, you will be shocked at the half-naked dress of our women, who say they want to look sexy. Some women rush in for breast implants just to get men's attention. It is not bad to admire a beautiful woman or parts of her body if it is just for the appreciation of God's beautiful creation. With a clean heart and without a lustful eye, anyone is free to say someone is a handsome man or beautiful woman. Any man who marries a woman just because of her breasts, legs, or other body part should know that before long, maybe in pregnancy or with age, they will begin to give way.

Familiarity may blind some men to what they have. They begin to think better, prettier women are available to them. This thinking, if not taken care of, may become a highway to marital unfaithfulness. You will always see beautiful women with seemingly better breasts, legs, and buttocks. When you get married, you do not become blind to other beautiful girls. But your marriage is in jeopardy if you begin to regret you do not have the most attractive woman as your wife.

No woman should be carried away by a man who sings the praises of her physical beauty. Unfortunately, women love to hear such compliments. Some women think something is wrong if no man tells them they are beautiful.

> Men are called upon to enjoy the wife of their youth and to enjoy their breast forever. May your fountain be blessed, and may you rejoice in the wife of your youth. A loving doe, a graceful deer may her breasts satisfy you always, may you ever be intoxicated with her love. (Prov. 5:18-19)

In this verse, we see the man must first glory in the totality of his wife before enjoying specific parts of her body. What if for medical reasons one or both of her breasts is cut off? Will you still cherish her and see her as your queen? What if she's in a serious fire or accident and her body is deformed? Will she still be treasured? Until you go to your grave, never say it cannot happen to you. One never knows what tomorrow will bring. If you feel you cannot accept her as a wife when one part of her body is taken off, don't marry her. Let her go to the person who will accept her in totality as a person.

Marrying to Have Children

This point sounds old school to many in the postmodern world. I hear this every day, "Who needs to get married before having children? Who needs a man to have a child?" A woman can go to the doctor's office and come back pregnant. Because of health complications, some may seek the help of science. When one boasts that he or she does not need to be married before having children, this simply shows how morally weak our communities have become. I also hear women say, "I am not getting younger. Menopause is around the corner, and I need to marry and have my babies." Many of our women marry as a fight against menopause; they struggle to bear children before menopause puts its hands on them. Marrying just because you want to have a child—because it is more dignified to be married before giving birth—is a very weak foundation. In each African marriage, childbearing plays a very important role. Even if it is not verbalized, it is in the mind of any African who marries.

This is not only a woman's problem. Men also think about having children. To some African men, if the baby is not a boy, it is not a child yet.

Children are good, but they should not be a primary reason for marrying. Some societies put great emphasis on having children.

> Children are the major concern of people; marriage that does not produce children is considered a failure. If you don't get married and have children, who will pour out libation to you when you die? Marriage is the focal point of all existence. Both the living and the departed together with those yet unborn meet together at this key point.[33]

Marrying someone because you want to have children is getting a children-producing machine. If the machine fails to do its job, it will be thrown away, and another will be gotten. Most often, it is believed an African man is never barren; it is always the problem of the woman. Women who cannot have children are often abused by her in-laws as not being a woman enough.

Most men who marry for the sake of children are good at premarital sexual intercourse. Their aim is to impregnate the woman before marriage. Women marrying

---

[33]   J. Gehman Richard, *African Traditional Religion* (Nyeri, Kenya: Kesho Publication, 1990), 53.

to bear children for their own glory will soon see no reason to stay in a marriage when they are unable to do what they came to do or after they have had children. If they stay in a marriage, it is to take care of their children. It is natural for all of us to desire dancing around with our biological children or grandchildren. But it should not be the main reason for marriage.

Children are a gift, an inheritance from God.

> Behold, children are a heritage from the Lord, the fruit of the womb a reward. Like arrows in the hand of a warrior are the children of one's youth. Blessed is the man who fills his quiver with them. He shall not be put to shame when he speaks with his enemies in the gate. (Ps. 127:3-5 ESV)

> And when Esau lifted up his eyes and saw the women and children, he said, "Who are these with you?" Jacob said, "The children whom God has graciously given your servant." (Gen. 33:5 ESV)

> He gives the barren woman a home, making her the joyous mother of children. Praise the Lord. (Ps. 113:9)

Even though most women will say they do not need to be married in the twenty-first century in order to bear children, we cannot refuse the fact that it was not so from the beginning. God the creator and the inventor of marriage and the giver of our sexual desires and the giver of children never intended from the very beginning that children begotten out of marriage. If God gives you, fine. If God does not, fine. He still loves you and cheers you on.

All My Friends Are Married

Marriage is not a competition. The fact that all your friends are married does not signal you need to rush into marriage. Some parents and elders in our churches are very good at using this to force their children to marry. Your friends may be married. Some may be younger than you are. Some may have lived very rough lives, yet they are married, and you are not. Do not force yourself to marry a person because your friends are all married. This is a weak foundation for a marriage. Marry when it is your time, but know the time is not in your keeping. God is keeping the time, and he is neither early nor late. If you wait on the Lord patiently, he will visit you in his time and for your happiness. God has not forgotten you. Keep on trusting him and believing in him.

He or She Is from a Rich Family

The Bible says it is easier for a camel to pass through the hole of a needle than for a rich man to enter heaven. This tells us something is terribly wrong with the life of a rich man who does not know Christ. If riches could buy love or make marriages stable, Hollywood marriages would be among the best in the world. The reverse seems to be true, despite all their money. The family or individual may be rich, but you may never enjoy the riches. People who marry for money seldom stay when times are hard. When the money is gone, they are gone.

I have seen many humble, honest, and selfless rich people. I have also seen humble and caring children from rich families, yet many believe the rich are very rude and immoral, without respect for anyone. Many African men will not marry a woman from a rich family. They complain that most are lazy, cannot cook, and do not respect their husbands. Their parents, because of money, will always want to control their son-in-law. Some men who dare to marry women from rich families do so for self-gratification and are always ready for a divorce.

In the diaspora, some women marry rich men with the idea that an issue will come up one day so they can use as a stepping-stone for divorce and a large financial settlement.

Marrying for Papers

The issue of immigration papers to live and work in a foreign land is not an easy matter among Africans in the diaspora. Many have gone through hell to get papers. From the beginning, this is real business, not marriage, and the road is rough. God help us. The experience is very painful. You work very hard, only to give the money to the person you are marrying for the sake of your immigration papers. The lawyer takes his own share of your money. It is said that in this business, the women are more demanding and troublesome than the men. When they want to make a new, expensive demand, the women threaten to drop or cancel the agreement. The Akata men and women know this is the only way they can tap money from struggling African men and women.

Without papers, you have nothing to say and no voice. You do not want to begin anew with another person, who may end up being worse. Besides, they are not always easy to find. With bitter tears, they give in, praying for the day the arranged marriage will be accepted and the green card received. I wish families in Africa could know the hell their children go through in order to have resident permits to live and work freely in the diaspora.

What really concerns us here is when Africans turn to play over others. It is very painful to meet an African who is already a citizen in the diaspora deceived by one who craftily presents himself or herself as an African angel, asking to marry him or her. But in these cases, in the back of his or her mind is the green card; that is all this "angel" wants. After getting the green card, the individual shows his or her true colors. He or she walks away shamelessly, causing someone to be called a divorcee, while he or she has never thought of ever bearing that name and possible stigma.

Even if you got married for a wrong reason, by the grace of God, that can be changed, and you can start living in your marital home for the right, healthy reasons. There is always hope when Christ Jesus is given the chance to lead a family.

Healthy Reasons for Marriage

If there are wrong reasons or foundations for marriage, there are right reasons, which many neglect. If there is a counterfeit, it is because the real thing exists. There are many healthy reasons for marriage, but I am presenting just a few. These few are able to pull others to them and keep marriage strong and steady for a lifetime.

To Glorify God

God does everything for his glory. He created the world and all that is in it for his glory. He created man and marriage for his glory. "Bring my sons from afar and my daughters from the end of the earth, everyone who is called by my name, whom I created for my glory" (Isa. 43:6). God is most glorified when man sets out to give him the due glory that he shares with no one.[31]

"So whether you eat or drink or whatever you do, do it all for the glory of God" (1 Cor. 10:31). "And whatever you do, whether in word or deed, do it all in the name of the Lord Jesus, giving thanks to God the Father through him" (Col. 3:17). One of the things to be done in the name of the Lord, for his glory, is marriage.

Marrying to glorify God is where we find our best weapon to protect marriage. The sanctity of marriage is uplifted when two believers in Christ step out to glorify God in marriage. As a consequence, the world will see God's glorious gift of marriage in their love. God can only be glorified if he is first in the marriage and if the marriage is in his will. Unfortunately, many do not seek the face of God for a life partner. Many of us in the diaspora do not know anything as the will of God. We have become too wise, too rich, and too important that no one cares to pray for a life partner. A wedding in a fancy church does not guarantee God's approval or his being in the marriage.

Putting God first in your marriage is very important, though not easy. Marriage is secondary and temporary, while God is primary and infinite. Marriages should always point us to God, the institutor of marriage. Our ancestors did not institute marriage. God, to whom all glory is due, did. To glorify God, we submit ourselves to him every day and do all he has asked us to do. That is living in obedience to the Word of God. He who obeys him is a wise builder who builds his house and family upon the Rock.

> Why do you call me, "Lord, Lord," and do not do what I say? I will show you what he is like who comes to me and hears my words and puts them into practice. He is like a man building a house, who dug down deep and laid the foundation on rock. When a flood came, the torrent struck that house but could not shake it, because it was well built. But the one who hears my words and does not put them into practice is like a man who built a house on the ground without a foundation. The moment the torrent struck that house, it collapsed and its destruction was complete." (Luke 6:46-49)

The Rock is Christ Jesus. God will do everything for his glory, which may include stopping you from marrying. So not all will marry, and it will be God's doing. If you marry, let it be for the glory of God. If you stay single after years of praying and fasting for a life partner, let him get the glory.

To Express the Relationship of Christ and His Church

In writing to the Ephesians about marriage, Paul could only liken it to the relationship between the church and Christ Jesus. The husband is called on to wash his wife with the Word to present her blameless on the day of Christ. He has to lead his family as Christ leads his church. Wives are told to be submissive to their husbands as unto the Lord. For the sake of Christ, the wife has to submit to her husband. He may not deserve it, but for the sake of Christ, she is called to do so. The only example of Christ's relationship with the church is marriage, so we should do everything to love like Christ and let our marriages reflect him and his glory.

To Fulfill Sexual Desires in a Godly Manner

The subject of sex is not a common one in African communities. The church is very silent, but Hollywood, the great Western ambassador to many corners of Africa, is not. Women of the church get pregnant every day, and the authors of the pregnancies are some of the men in church. This indicates the church has to speak out clearly about marriage and sex. Unfaithful African men are good at pointing to King David and King Solomon as examples, forgetting the consequences. Almost all African men in the diaspora were taught to think they are free to have as many wives as they can, or to have sex with any woman of their choice anytime they want. This may be one of the reasons HIV/AIDS is so prevalent in Africa.

It is important to know that human sexuality is one of the most precious gifts God has given to men and women. The fact it is a gift from God is not the problem. The problem arises from when and how this gift is to be enjoyed. The Devil, who has nothing and gives nothing to anyone, distorts the concept of this gift in the minds of men and women. The talk we hear everywhere is, "God gave me to use it for my enjoyment, so I have to enjoy it now with whomever, wherever, and however I want." This is certainly an abuse of the gift, not enjoyment. As God is angry with homosexual relations, he is equally angry with people having premarital and extramarital sex. Sex before and out of marriage is sinful and ungodly and punishable by God, the giver of all good gifts. The joy is that it is a forgivable sin if one confesses and turns away from it.

Having marital sex between a man and a woman is not sinful and has never been sinful. The sin of Adam and Eve in the garden of Eden was not a sex sin, despite what many believe. Some go around saying the genital area of the human body is in the middle, where the tree was. If the Bible tells the whole world the sexual sins of David, Tama, Judah, and even that of Lot with his daughters, why would it not tell us that of Adam and Eve? Would God have ceased being God? Sex in marriage is an act of worship, and God is glorified when he watches a husband and wife in the act. Wherever and whenever you have sex, know God is watching you. If you got married before having sex, you did not miss anything. If you are abstaining from sex now because you want to have it only when you are married, you are not missing anything. It is your pride and your dignity. Do not let bad friends and the boyfriend and girlfriend madness in the diaspora mislead you. Marriage is deeper than just having sex that is why many people will not marry those they are doing that with. Do not think that giving yourself sexually to a boy will make him to marry you. But when you get into the depths of marriage which is in Christ Jesus that is when you really enjoy sex. Women who sincerely love marriage will desire men they know are not messing around. Not so with the women. Sadly, the bad men will compete with each other to see who will bring down the woman they know is not going out with any man. They use all the tactics available to them to get her. If they cannot come in through the door, they will try to use the window. My sisters, you need to stand firm in Christ and for Christ. Just as it is not good to steal food because you are hungry, so it is not good to fulfill your sexual desires in an unfaithful and ungodly manner. Only in marriage can sexual desire be fulfilled in a godly manner between one man and one woman.

To Begin a Family

The family is very important to God. One person cannot make a family. It takes two opposite sexes to make a family. That is why God made man and woman. You do not make a family by having children out of wedlock. Homosexual couples cannot make a family. Human organizations and governments may approve of same-sex marriage, but in truth, two people of the same gender cannot make a family as God wanted it to be. It is not in his will. They may adopt children, but it will never be a family. God brings a Christian woman and a Christian man together in marriage that they may build up a godly family.

Marriage creates the best environment for raising children. "The Lord is acting as the witness between you and your wife, because you have broken faith with her, even though she is your partner, the wife of your marriage covenant. Has not the Lord made them one? In flesh and spirit, they are his, because he seeks godly offspring. So guard yourself in your spirit, and do not break faith with your wife" (Malachi 2:14-15).

For Companionship

You can have companions everywhere in life. You can have a work, church, or school companion. But true, deep, and lasting companionship can only be gained in marriage.

Companionship is living life together, working together toward a common vision, and sharing your joys, victories, and failures together as one. Companionship is the ability to share your life with another person on a daily basis. A very important ingredient to companionship is communication. Unfortunately, many marriages do not have this element of companionship, and marriages void of the spirit of companionship easily fall apart.

If you know you are going to share your lifetime with someone, you need to think well before asking a woman, "Will you marry me?" And the woman must think long and hard before saying yes.

CHAPTER 4

Things to Think about before You Ask, "Will You Marry Me?" and before You Answer, "Yes, I Will"

H uman beings are good at rushing into many things, but marriage should not be one of them. Unfortunately, many do rush into marriage every day. Africans in Africa and the diaspora do not know how to prepare themselves for an upcoming event. They wait until the eve of the program, and they start rushing in and out. African football teams may not perform well in World Cup competitions, especially the one that just took place in Africa, due to lack of preparation.

Undoubtedly, one reason for the failure of African marriages in the diaspora is also a lack of preparation. Many couples rush into marriage without thinking. Some believe the best way to prepare for marriage is to cohabit, yet studies show a good percentage of marriages after cohabitation did not last long.

Rushing to ask a woman's hand in marriage is very dangerous. Because it is almost a universal tradition for the man to ask a woman to marry, it is very important he gives much thought about the woman he is considering. He should ask people whose opinions he respects about her. When the boy makes up his mind and asks the woman to marry him, he should give her time to think and pray about it. Though she should not rush to respond, the woman should not keep stalling the man. When a man, especially the one who is not messing around with other women, decides to marry, he does not want to be delayed.

There are many things to think about before marrying. I would love the couple to think about the following things before asking and before saying yes.

Am I Comfortable with the Totality of His or Her Physical Appearance?

Many of us from African tribes were made to believe that a woman is a woman or a man is a man. You do not have to care about their appearance. Some men believe beautiful women are not submissive and always unfaithful. Some women think the same; you cannot have a handsome man alone, for he will surely be unfaithful. Some women fighting menopause will not let go of any man who comes by at this time, which they consider a crossroads in their lives. They say to themselves, *I have waited for the handsome ones to come, but they did not. Though not good looking, I will manage him.* She gets married, and after some time, she abuses the man with these painful words no man or woman wants to hear: "I just managed you. There are better men out there."

The issue of appearance has many debates. I am not talking about what others say about the appearance of the person you are considering for marriage. He may be handsome to you, but not to your sisters or your brothers. On the other hand, she may be beautiful to you but not to your friends, mother, or others. The physical appearance of your spouse gives you extra confidence among your friends and the opposite sex at work, church, and so forth. Let your eyes be satisfied with what they see before you check the person's character. When Adam first saw Eve, what he saw moved him, and he said, "She is flesh of my flesh and bone of my bones" (Gen. 2:22-23). Though flesh of my flesh and bone of my bones may have a deeper meaning, in this context I am using it as the physical person Adam saw and loved so deeply. It was that which he was able to hold in his arms and be satisfied with.

Here is my advice if you are about to marry and cannot imagine enjoying yourself in the arms of the person or sitting in the town hall meeting with her or him. Think again. If you cannot imagine yourself joyfully walking side by side on the street or into a family meeting, think about your decision all over again, even if he or she has good Christian character. The person may not be the right one for you. As far as I am concerned, handsomeness, beauty, and good character must move together.

Are We Compatible?

Sexual and emotional compatibility should not be overlooked. Compatibility is the ability to live together in harmony. Even if you are not thinking of compatibility, God does. When God was telling himself that he would make for Adam a suitable helper, he was talking about compatibility. You cannot be a suitable helper until you are compatible. What values do both of you have in common? Check if you are sexually compatible. It sounds funny, but it is very important. It is not through having premarital sex. Talk freely about your sex life before getting married. If you are unable to bring up the subject, your pastor or marriage counselor can help both of you shamelessly talk about your sex life and even how many children you want, even if God will bless you with any. Check to see how frequently you want sex. Does he or she want to have sex every day, while you want sex once every two weeks or so? You do not have to walk around this, because incompatibility in this area is a red flag that your marriage could be in danger.

Emotions compatibility: Emotion can be said to be a state of mind stemming from one's circumstances and mood. This state of mind is easily carried away by things like joy, anger, love and hate. You want to find out if the things that make you laugh are the things that make your spouse angry. What are his or her fears and are there the things you fear also? Is he or she emotionally stable? How does he or she handle crises? Is he one who will not eat or talk with you because of one thing out of many that builds a relationship? If you people are emotionally compatable then you may also be socially compatable having lots of things in common. This will help you to enjoy each other fully.

Will My Life Dreams Be Accomplished in the Relationship?
Marriage is not a dream killer. People should be able to still pursue their dreams after marriage. Each partner should be ready to help the other see his or her dreams come true. For this to happen, you have to think about your dreams and those of your intended spouse before getting married. Ask yourself, *Will my progress in life be a threat to the person I am about to marry? Will the person support me to move on with the dreams I had for life before getting married?*

I met a pastor planning to marry a woman studying international relations. In the course of our discussion, I asked the woman, "What do you intend to do after your studies?"

She said, "Work with the UN and move around."

I then asked her, "Does that vision move hand in hand with your plans to marry a pastor?"

Her answer was, "I have never thought of that."

They left my house, and the next thing I heard, was that she ended the engagement because her dreams did not match those of the pastor. She does not hate the pastor, but what she wants to do in life is far from compatible with being a pastor's wife. A pastor's wife can do many things, but this she cannot. Both marriage and your dreams for life are good. It's bad when you get married and then begin to regret you are unable to become what you have always wanted. Regrets are not good for any marriage.

What Does He or She Think about Marriage?
Knowing the person's views about marriage is very important. Why is the person marrying you? Is marriage valuable to him or her? Is marriage something worth protecting? Does the person think marriage will stop him or her from jumping all over the place? Is your intended spouse trying to get settled, or are his or her parents forcing a marriage to settle down the person? Marriage does not settle people. Settled and mature persons get into marriage. Does he or she respect marriage as God does, believing that marriage is a lifetime commitment between a man and woman? Does he or she respect the opposite sex? Is he one who asks, "What is a woman?" Or is she one who will ask, "What is a man?"

Has He or She been Divorced?
Among Africans, a divorced man will easily get another woman, but not so with a woman. A family may allow their divorced son to get married to a young, virgin woman but will not allow their son to marry a divorced woman. Divorced women go through several checkpoints and scans before they are accepted. Many good people who love marriage are divorced because the other party forced it on them. Still, it is good to find out what happened. Do not forget you are getting only one side of the conversation, and most speakers will defend themselves. As you talk, look for red flags. If the man was the problem, you will soon walk out like the first, second, and third women before you. If the woman was the problem, you will soon begin to see red flags. No red flag sign should be minimized.

I would love to say a divorced person should take some time to heal himself or herself before getting into another serious relationship. When you decide to marry a divorced person, you will sometimes get some kicks meant for the person who hurt your spouse in the first marriage. Sometimes your spouse will look at you but see the person who hurt him or her. This shows healing and forgiveness have not taken place.

My traditional background does not believe in divorce. Some years ago, a woman's parents would tell her the oracles say that she should never go to their compound or home, because if she did, her children, she, or even one of her parents would die. This would keep the poor woman in an abusive, brutal marriage. My religious background carries the same message. My religion says marriage is for "better or for worse." I am still searching for the biblical book, chapter, and verse that say we marry for better or worse. I do not want to say it is not biblical, because I may have just not found it yet. This "for better or for worse" nonsense has kept many of our women in inhumane, abusive situations not fit to be called marriage. When she shares her pain with her pastor or elders, they only tell her, "Remember, you got married for better or for worse." I have heard a devil incarnate man tell his battered wife, "You married me for better or for worse." I am not encouraging divorce, but am encouraging a Christ-centered life-style that will make your spouse never to dream of divorce. Still we are living in a fallen world.

If a divorced person wants to marry you, think wisely and ask the right questions. If you decide to marry him or her, make sure you do not use the previous marriage to abuse him or her. Do not come to regret why you married a divorced person. It is better to be a single than to be married but regret why you got married.

Is He or She a Friendly Person?

"A man that hath friends must show himself friendly and there is a friend that sticketh closer than a brother" (Prov. 18:24).

Two are better than one, because they have a good return for their work. If one falls, his or her friend can help the person up. But pity the one who falls and has no one to help him or her up! Also, if two lie down together, they will keep warm. But how can one alone keep warm? Though one may be overpowered, two can defend themselves. A cord of three strands is not quickly broken (Eccles. 4:9-12).

> A friend loves at all times, and a brother is born for adversity. (Prov. 17:17).

> A man of many companions may come to ruin, but there is a friend who sticks closer than a brother. (Prov. 18:24)

> There is no greater love than to lay down one's life for one's friends. You are my friends if you do what I command. I no longer call you slaves, because a master doesn't confide in his slaves. Now you are my friends, since I have told you everything the Father told me. (John 15:13-15)

> As iron sharpens iron, so a friend sharpens a friend. (Prov. 27:17)

The heartfelt counsel of a friend is as sweet as perfume and incense. (Prov. 27:9)

A friend is always loyal, and a brother is born to help in time of need. (Prov. 17:17)

The godly give good advice to their friends; the wicked lead them astray. (Prov. 12:26)

It is believed a friendly person will be a good spouse. Does he or she have problems wherever he or she goes and with everyone around him or her? The person you are considering for marriage must be your closest friend. When all others are gone, he or she will still be a friend to you.

Does He or She Have Children Out of Wedlock?

I heard of an instance where a woman made her son call her "sister," so no one would ever know he was her son. Men do the same thing in keeping their out-of-wedlock children far away from the knowledge of their wives.

Children born out of wedlock, as any other child, are blessings from God. It happened in the past, and there is no need to keep it a secret. If you had a child out of wedlock, it is good to tell your future spouse about the child. If he or she accepts you and the child, fine. If not, both of you can find ways to deal with the situation or call off the marriage. He or she may never become the parent of the child, but for the health of the relationship, the child should be accepted as part of the family if both of you still want to marry.

How Does He or She Treat Money?

Many people do not know how to handle money. Some just love to keep money. They glory in banking money but have no shoes or anything to eat. Some have debts everywhere, and you never know what they did with the money. They never stay at home until the paycheck is gone. This person is not ready for marriage. Imagine the shame upon you when people call your home every day, asking for the money your spouse owes them. Thank God few Africans spend money carelessly in the diaspora, because each person struggles with a project back home.

What Is the Overall Character of This Person?

So many people are attracted to their mates because of their personality. Just because he makes you laugh, should not be a determining factor for true love and a happy marriage. Look for character, not personality. The person's character shows how you and your children will be treated. The heat of marital crisis can easily melt personality, but character is the substance that stands the test of time. Find out if the person is God-fearing, trustworthy, respectful, responsible, fair, and caring.

Am I Comfortable with His or Her Culture, Race, Ethnicity, and Religious Affiliation?

Many people overlook this area only to later realize it is hindering the joy of their marriage. Even if you met in the diaspora, culture and religion do influence marriage. If you do not approve of his religion, it will be difficult to live with him. We should know that no culture is better than another. Talking about the negative aspects of your spouse's culture in an unfriendly manner kills love. It is always good to seek counsel and know something about the culture of the people marriage is leading you to join. Marriage is not something you should go into blindly. In fact, love is not really blind, as it is commonly said. You do have to think and ask questions before getting into any serious relationship. Even if both of you believe in the Lord Jesus Christ, you still have to ask these questions.

If you have decided to marry someone from the Western culture, you need to give it deep thought. Know that you are going to relinquish many things, especially if you are an African man marrying a Western woman. In every marriage, both parties have to adjust their worldview and beliefs, but it is very difficult for a white woman to adjust in any way to being like an African woman. She sits in her world and waits for the African man to adjust and meet her in her world. Above all, there is always the belief that the Western culture is far better. Do not think that because he or she is an African American that he thinks and reasons like someone from Africa. Know that your worldviews are worlds apart. The cultural gulf is wide, deep, and frightening. It may not pinch you in the beginning, but you have to think and think again when it comes to marriage. No matter how well you think you have integrated into the Western or African culture, think and think again. Do not allow your emotions to outsmart your judgment and critical thinking.

Is He or She God's Will for Me?

Knowing the will of God for a life partner is not easy. Some Africans in the diaspora do not really care about the will of God as to whom they should marry. In fact, some really do not care about God. The women back home in Africa, together with their parents, also do not care to seek the will of God. The moment they hear the man is in the diaspora, it is automatically the will of God. The man in the diaspora just has to see a picture of a woman he knew in college or elementary school and who is now ready for marriage. Sometimes the man goes home for a few weeks to search for marriageable women. Before the time is over, he has already chosen one of the women for marriage without any prayer for the will of God. For people such as this, God is known only when things are bad. God, whose advice was never sought, is blamed for all the bad things that happen in the marriage.

A woman shared with me how she made the worst mistake of her life when she married an unbeliever. When she was tortured and abused in marriage, she cried out to God, blaming him for all she was going through. God said to her, "You did not ask me for a life partner. I did not choose your spouse for you. I did not give him to you." God may be saying this to many in the diaspora who are crying and blaming him. I am not saying that if God verbally makes his will very clear to you by saying, "Ngong, this is your wife, and you, Bih, this is your husband," you will never face marital crisis. The will of God does not guarantee freedom from crisis, but it does gives courage and confidence to work things out.

The importance of seeking God's will for a life partner can never be overemphasized. Each of us is unique, and so is every marriage and family. God made us unique and deals with us in our uniqueness. The way God gave me my wife is not the way he will give yours to you. God will treat you uniquely, because you are unique. Our uniqueness makes it very difficult for anyone to devise a formula on how to know who your life partner may be. Some pastors tell their young people to ask for signs. They get this from Genesis 24, where Abraham's servant asked for a sign to know the woman God chose for Isaac.

> What is here for you and I to learn is not the asking for a sign but the fact that we have to trust God and have faith in him in all situations. If you choose to ask for a sign, know that Satan is also very good at producing counterfeit signs that may look just like what you asked God. Remember what happened with Moses in Egypt. The Egyptian sorcerers and magicians were able to produce counterfeit snakes. (Exod. 7:8-13)

If you ask for a white cap, do not forget there are many kinds of white. Living in accordance with the already revealed will of God in the Bible leads to the possibility of marrying in the will of God. If you forsake the will of God, do not think you will be able to know his will just when it comes to marriage.

> "For I know the plans I have for you," declares the Lord, "plans to prosper you and not to harm you, plans to give you hope and a future. Then you will call on me and come and pray to me, and I will listen to you. You will seek me and find me when you seek me with all your heart." (Jer. 29:11-13)

> It is God's will that you should be sanctified: that you should avoid sexual immorality. (1 Thess. 4:3)

> It is God's revealed will that you make his word your lamp. Your word is a lamp for my feet, a light on my path. It is God's revealed will that you seek first his kingdom. (Ps. 119:105).

> But seek ye first the kingdom of God, and his righteousness; and all these things shall be added unto you. (Matt. 6:33)

It is God's will that the renewing of your mind transform you.

I beseech you therefore, brethren, by the mercies of God, that ye present your bodies a living sacrifice, holy, acceptable unto God, which is your reasonable service. And be not conformed to this world but be ye transformed by the renewing of your mind, that ye may prove what is that good, and acceptable, and perfect, will of God. For I say, through the grace given unto me, to every man that is among you, not to think of himself more highly than he ought to think; but to think soberly, according as God hath dealt to every man the measure of faith. (Rom. 12:1-3)

It is God's revealed will that we diligently obey his commands.

> But take diligent heed to do the commandment and the law, which Moses the servant of the Lord charged you, to love the Lord your God, and to walk in all his ways, and to keep his commandments, and to cleave unto him, and to serve him with all your heart and with all your soul. (Josh. 22:5)

It is God's will that we delight in him.

> Delight thyself also in the Lord: and he shall give thee the desires
> of thine heart. Rest in the Lord, and wait patiently for him. (Ps.
> 37:4, 7a)

CHAPTER 5

The Destroyers of African Marriages
in the Diaspora

A fricans in the diaspora have become very complicated, making it difficult to put a finger on the things that are destroying their marriages. For the time I have been in the diaspora teaching and preaching the Gospel I have realized that the following few can be found in three of five divorce cases of Africans in the diaspora.

False Identification

False identification is just another name for manipulation. As a pastor, I have listened to couples in crisis in both Africa and the diaspora. In some, I find disappointments stemming from false identification and manipulation. You do not always see disappointment displayed obviously in a marriage. You need to dig a little deeper to see that one of the spouses has felt manipulated from the very beginning of the relationship. False identification comes from poor self-esteem and lack of self-confidence. What you get through manipulation is not yours and may never be yours. You may have it but shall never enjoy it.

It is painful to say some people foolishly, for whatever reasons, do not tell their partners in Africa the true story of how it is in industrialized countries. They describe the West as a blissful and trouble-free world, making those back in Africa to wrongfully believe it is paradise on earth. When they finally join them in the diaspora and they cannot get jobs, hard as they try, and their partner's earnings are not enough to provide the comfort they dreamed of while in Africa, they become disappointed and start developing a plan B.

Unfortunately, most plan Bs are unhealthy for a family. Emmanuel Sarpong gives us a very clear example of false identification and manipulation, which I paraphrase here.

> A Ghanaian woman once said that while she was still living in Ghana, one Ghanaian man living in Britain returned to Ghana and met her there some years ago. The man told her how he had become a British man, working with one of the high-ranking companies in the United Kingdom and making big money in the company. After having exalting himself at home, he got into a relationship with the girl before leaving for Britain. After some time, the girl got a visa to study in Britain. Hoping to marry this man, she moved in to live with him. After a few months, she found out that the man does not even have British passport and is not a British citizen as he bragged. He does not have work authorization. He was using another man's documents to work in a warehouse. The woman realized her plan to marry this guy was nothing but chasing the wind. Was there any reason for this guy to tell all the lies he told this woman? Africans in the diaspora do not give people back home the right information about the hardship of life in the Western world. They fear that they will not be respected and given a red carpet reception if they tell the truth about their sleepless struggles in the diaspora.
>
> First things first. If anyone is planning for their spouses to join them in the diaspora, tell them everything about yourself and how hard and fast life is in the diaspora. Give them the true picture of what they will face. Let them know that life is not for lazy people in the diaspora. If it is possible, let a clergyperson or an elder aware of what Africans are going through in the diaspora give them a good orientation before they travel to meet you wherever you may be in the diaspora. This will help regulate their expectations and prepare their minds to accept what they will face in the diaspora.[34]

---

[34]   www.ghanaweb.com/GhanaHomePage/diaspora/artikel.php?ID=212945.

The answer to Emmanuel's question is simple. You do not have to say you are fine while you are not. You cannot lose what you do not have. It is all made up, and it does not take long for the truth to come out that you are not who or what you claim to be. If you are a security officer in America, do not tell a woman in your native country that you are general manager of a company in America. When she comes and meets you in your security uniform, she will be disappointed and may never trust you again. Many Africans in the diaspora make people back home think one can pick dollars off the streets in America. They spend years struggling, gathering money just to go home and play big. What is the gain in it?

It is false identity when you:

- Claim to be rich
- Claim to have no problem getting money while you are barely surviving
- Pretend to be one who never gets angry

Many single persons are good at hiding their true character, but when they are finally married, their true colors come out. There is no need to present a false identity to your wife—or husband-to-be. You can pretend to a passerby, but not to someone you hope to spend the rest of your life with. But because the world has become a global village, there is no need for that. Those who do this are setting time bombs for themselves. The painful truth is when it explodes, children, friends, and other family members will be affected.

Pressures from In-Laws

In-law problems and relationships cannot all be painted with the same brush. The solutions to them are unique and filled with as much variety as the people they represent. Your in-laws are an intricate and basic part of your spouse's life. In-laws, in many ways, represent an unacknowledged, undefined web of relationships. As an in-law or would-be in-law, you have a space to fill, and you have to decide what will fill the space: friendly words, kind and loving acts, and caring behavior—or bitter words and unkind and unwelcoming behavior.[35]

Mother-in-law

Many men are Mama's boys. "He is my son." If you are married to a man who is the only son or the apple of his family's eye, know that you are likely marrying a mama's boy. Your mother-in-law will have a lot of controlling power in your marriage. Most

---

[35] Call Gloria Horsley, *The In-Law Survival Manuel* (Chichester: John Wiley & Sons, Inc., 1997), 3-5.

mothers glory in their only sons and only daughters and in their mind, no girl is fit to take care of their only son and no man is fit enough to take care of their only daughter. The bond between them is very strong. So when you see your mother-in-law stepping in, you do not have to fight back. Simply present yourself as a daughter. Be the daughter she has always wished to have. A mother-in-law can build as well as destroy marriages. It all depends on the limits the man sets.

Sister-in-law

"He is my brother." Sisters-in-law, especially the unmarried ones or those who did not make it in their own marriages, can be very dangerous. They are good at trying to watch over their brothers. Those in the West still want their brothers' wives to behave toward them as if they were in a little village in Africa. They note everything their brother's wife wears. To them, their brother's wife is nothing but a gold digger. Those in Africa think all the money is their brother's money, even if the woman earns more money than the brother does. Unfortunately, most African men listen to their sisters more than to their wives.

Some women take matters in their hands from the first day of marriage. They do not want their husbands to do anything to help their families. She talks about bringing her mother to the diaspora. After that, she talks about filing for her brother to come. She sends all nice things to her family and blocks anything going to her husband's family. When her husband struggles and gets one of his sisters or brothers to join them in the diaspora, the wife develops a program for all-night talking and complains about the husband's sister and brother. The only good people in the world are in her family. It is terrible trying to separate your husband from his family or your wife from hers.

An extended family relationship is very difficult to maintain but should never be neglected. These very good African values are worth preserving. Unfortunately, in-laws far and near have ruined many marriages in the diaspora. In the other hand some men are extremely wicked they mal-treat their wives together with their parents. How can you mal-treat your wife and exspect her relations to respect you?

A Clash of Cultures

A clash of cultures is when two or more cultures are in loggerhead, disagreeing on their beliefs and lifestyle. Misunderstanding and disagreements between different cultures cause the clash. The vast differences between the African and Western cultures are breaking marriages. I have heard many people say the major factor behind divorce among Africans is the impact of the new American culture. Africans in America stumble on the American culture of rights, and in many cases, do not know how to handle it. We know African societies are male dominated, and men have more rights than women. In a typical African family, the woman plays domestic roles, while the man is the breadwinner. Women do household work, raise the kids, and serve their husbands.

In America, African women find:

- They have rights just like men and perhaps more than men.
- They hold important nondomestic jobs and are financially strong, just like the men.
- They have equal say on issues in the home and are able to financially contribute.

These empowered women often overlook their African cultural values. Some go to the extreme of making culturally inexpedient demands on their husbands, because they make more money. Others go so far as usurping their husband's role as the head of the family. African men hate some of these rights and reject them with all bitterness. African men see Western culture of rights a challenge to their masculinity. In some cases, their reactions lead to tension in the family that soon causes marital problems. Many of these marital problems lead to divorce. Certainly many other factors lead to the high rate of divorce among Africans in the diaspora; however, the American culture of rights seems to be at the top of the list.

In the Western culture, achievements are not venerated. Nobody cares to know what you have acquired. A highly respected general director in Africa will find that he or she has no place in this culture. Things the man has never done in his African culture, the Western culture forces on him. Maybe he has never washed dashes, cooked food, or taken care of the trash. In the West, he has to do them. All the glories and honors your culture gave you are gone. Little kids will come and ask how old you are. They will call you directly by your first name, without any Mr., Uncle, or Mrs. I was surprised when a twelve-year-old boy turned and called a grandfather of about eighty-six years by his first name. Because I had only been in the diaspora a few days, I almost asked the boy if he were out of his mind. After my family joined me in the diaspora, we went to church on Sunday morning, and a seven-year-old girl called me by my first name in the presence of my little sons. My son of the same age as the little girl could not believe it. I could see the surprise on his face. He had never heard anyone call his father carelessly like that.

Another thing that surprised me (and I know it does the same to most Africans new in the diaspora) is the number of women smokers in the West. And this despite the fact smoking in general has become frowned upon in Western culture. Culture is learned from childhood. Now in the West, one has to become a little child in order to learn how to cope in the Western culture. Woman and children are naturally gifted to adjust easily and accept their new environment. It is not so with men. They experience much regret that they have to change. Sometimes our wives in the West want us to adjust as quickly as they have, and this may lead to marital crisis, which may slowly lead to divorce.

I am not advocating for any culture here, for there are weaknesses in all of them. I hope that we live like believers in Christ Jesus. In Christ, we humble ourselves and depend on each other for the glory of God and our happiness.

The Spirit of Independence

This spirit of independence comes mostly from some African women in the diaspora. When they join their husbands in the diaspora, they feel as if they are in heaven after their green cards have been issued and they are sure of a regular paycheck. With their papers in their hands and assurance they will be protected by the Western law—which some feel favors women—these women, who were very humble in Africa, develop teeth and claws and are ready to devour. In the quest to live her own life, she starts seeing nothing good in her husband. She drives and goes wherever she wants. She comes back whenever she wants and dresses the way she wants. Her words become very poisonous, and her actions are geared to provoke her husband's anger. Her phone is always ready to call 9-1-1 the moment her husband, who might not have known her sexually for long, points a finger at her.

Whatever papers you have, resident permit or citizenship, you are an African by blood, not by a piece of paper. This spirit of independence is very bad. If we can kill this spirit in our communities, we will reduce the rate of divorce among Africans in the diaspora. A man or woman will never be independent of his or her spouse. We need each other all the time.

Verbal and Emotional Abuse

Verbal abuse is the habitual use of critical, sarcastic, and mocking words meant to put someone down either when alone or in front of others. Verbal abuse cannot be as easily identified as physical abuse. In the diaspora, many African men and women have resolved to verbally abuse their spouses. Sometimes words are more destructive than physical abuse. A physical wound from an abusive spouse can healed, but a wound in the heart caused by abusive words may cause pain for a lifetime. Abusive words can totally demoralize one. These days, the most painful and shameful words are often those spouses use to call their spouse derogative names and to intimidate and humiliate them. "I picked you . . ." "Dirty thing . . ." "I washed you . . ." "You think you are a man . . ." "You madwoman . . ." "You are a fool . . ." "Good for nothing." Screaming and not talking to your spouse is not helpful in any way. When these types of words are heard and the actions are seen repeatedly in a marriage, it is obvious the union is in serious trouble. The marriage is sick and needs healing. The marriage needs serious attention. Love, together with trust, has evaporated from the marriage. They have drifted away from their first love. The marriage can be healed only when one decides to behave maturely by forgiving the other. A struggle to keep peace in a marriage is a sign of maturity, not weakness and defeat.

We are so far away from home, and your spouse should be the closest person to you. If you only dream that you are abusing your spouse, please get up and pray against it. It is a bad dream. If Africans in the diaspora can put aside this bad habit of running down each other, it will be well with all of us. Whatever happens, remember to choose your words, knowing that one day you shall give an account to God of any careless words that came out of your mouth.

Work and Money, the Complex Pair

Each African who leaves his or her homeland does so with the idea of making big money. He or she is ready to do whatever comes that will give him or her money. Life in the diaspora is not easy, so the couple has to plan their jobs and how to spend their money. Work and money are complex pairs, because you cannot do without them. But on the other hand, if they are not well handled, they will kill you and your marriage. Some people work three jobs to keep up with life in the diaspora and the projects back home. Each leaves one job and connects to the next without going home.

When you talk about Christ and the need to worship, it sounds strange to many. What you hear is, "I do not have the time. I work Saturdays and Sundays. I have to pay my bills. Church is business. After all, I did not come here to go to church. I came to make money. I am only trying to help myself, for the Bible says that heaven helps those who help themselves."

This satanic saying is not found in the Bible. It is clear from the fall of man in the Garden of Eden in Genesis to the book of Revelation that heaven (God) helps those who cannot help themselves, for without Jesus, who is the true vine on whom we must abide, we can do nothing. Some who try to go to church will choose one where they will have little or no financial or spiritual commitment.

It becomes worse when the family has divided goals and dreams and when the family has teenagers to care for. The man is building mighty houses in his village. He also wants to get the title of a chief in his village, and he is struggling with a car loan.

The wife may be working hard to renovate her father's house back home without the knowledge of her husband, because most women will always think of their fathers first. She does everything to break the cycle of poverty in her family. For those with well-to-do parents, she thinks of other things to help lift the load of responsibility from her father's shoulders. She wants to send her brother to school or help him start a business that may end up being nothing but a ghost business. Her parents see money coming every two weeks or every month, and increase their demands even more.

I realize most parents back in Africa do not really care to know how their children make money in the diaspora. They only want money for building projects and drive cars sent home to them. How you get the money is not their problem. Some parents who personally sent their daughters to the diaspora before they got married will go so far as to encourage their daughters to divorce when they realize their husbands are keeping a close eye on how much their daughters make in a month and how they spend the money. It will be a great mistake to think that some parents whose daughters were taken to the diaspora by their husbands do not also encourage them to divorce their husbands and send them money. This is very sad. God help us.

Some African men who got their wives in Africa thought when the wives joined them in the diaspora, they would help them to pay all the money spent in helping them come over. Others helped their wives go to nursing schools while they remained security guards, hoping their wives would give them their paycheck when they start working.

This type of thinking is nothing but a poison that will kill your marriage. Most African women will not easily give their paychecks to their husbands and find it very hard to pay rent. Most African women, no matter their level of education and their large salaries, still believe men should meet all the financial responsibilities of the house. When she becomes involved with the financial issues of the house, she thinks she is a roommate, not a wife. She asks herself, *Why should I pay part of the rent and other bills?* It is something she did in school or at university with her roommates, dreaming to get married and enjoy the husband and his money. Some may buy food. But in the diaspora, with lots of financial demands from her family back home, she finds herself divided and pushed to a corner. She often chooses to send a good percentage of what she earns to her family and struggles to pay her house expenses and school loans with what remains.

African men should know they can't command their wives to give them money. Saying, "You must be giving me some amount of money every month," doesn't work. The African woman believes it is right for her husband to spend on her and should seek no refunds. Even if your wife earns more than you do, do not forget that she desires your money more than hers. African men in the diaspora should also know that an African woman will find it very hard to give her husband a dollar if she knows he is cheating on her. If you are paying child support, you need several skills to get money from your wife. And if she gives you money, expect some bitter words from her in the future.

In the diaspora, family responsibilities are shared fifty-fifty between the husband and his wife. If an African man fails to handle this well, the woman will start to think she is not valued. Let the African man tell his wife that he knows:

- He is the head of the family.
- He is responsible for the smooth running of the family.
- He is willing to supply all the needs of the family.

He is willing to pay all the bills, but the means are not there. That is why he seeks her financial help. If she gives little, do not argue. Take it and struggle on to make her see your sincere struggles. African women are very compassionate and will do their best to help a husband who realizes their worth, one who honors and respects them, one who has involved them in other issues, seeking their opinions and contributions in other family matters, not only in the paying of bills and rents in the diaspora. Thank God some African women are doing their very best in the hands of their very selfish, very stingy, self-centered husbands. Do not play with monetary issues, for they can destabilize your marriage for life. Money is either the best or worst area of communication in a marriage.[36]

During his earthly ministry, Jesus Christ spoke about money more than any other topic. He gave several warnings when he talked about Lazarus and the rich man, and his encounter with the rich young man. He tells us that even though man needs

---

[36] James Dobson, *Love for a Life Time* (Sisters, Ore.: Multnomah Books, 1993), 68.

bread, he cannot live by bread alone but by every word that comes from the mouth of the Lord. There is no profit in trying to gain or possess the whole world. For what will a man gain if he gains the whole word and loses his soul? A man's life does not consist in the abundance of his possessions (Matt. 4:4, 6:21, 1:26; Luke 12:15).

Apostle Paul comes in with more warnings on the love of money.

> Those who want to get rich fall into temptation and a trap and into many foolish and harmful desires that plunge people into ruin and destruction. For the love of money is a root of all kinds of evil. Some people, eager for money, have wandered from the faith and pierced themselves with many griefs. (1 Tim. 6:9-10)

> But mark this; there will be terrible times in the last days. People will be lovers of themselves, lovers of money, boastful, proud, abusive, disobedient to their parents, ungrateful, unholy. (2 Tim. 3:1-2)

Looking at our community today, centuries after Jesus Christ and the apostle Paul, we can clearly see the reasons for the hard warnings about the dangers of the love of money. Humankind has lusted for money, some have killed others because of money, and some have died in search of money. We cannot doubt that some might have gone to hell because of money.

Money has torn millions of marriages asunder and may destroy your marriage as well if you do not repent. Money has come between best friends. It has brought down the proud and mighty. More than any other thing, materialism has devastated more marriages and has kept families permanently and bitterly divided, even after those who labored, gathered, and built the houses have moved on to glory.

Many elderly Africans in the diaspora do say they are in there because of their children. But when you look carefully, you will find they are not in the diaspora for the better future of their kids. The fact that they are so devoted to their jobs and their quest to make money, leaving teenagers alone at home in the diaspora, speaks volumes. Some have worked, worked, and worked just to realize at the end that the wild winds of the diaspora have carried away their children and families.

Do not sacrifice your marriage and your children on the altar of work and money. No matter how successful you may be, all becomes nothing if your home is broken. Be careful that you do not spend all the time working to earn money for your family just to discover there is no family behind you at the end of everything.

False Expectations

Almost everyone goes into a marriage relationship with very high expectations. But we have to be realistic in our expectations. Many African men return to Africa for wives after they have frustrated African girls in the diaspora with false promises of marriage. They do so with the expectation that any girl from home will be so appreciative, submissive, and thankful to the man who gave them the opportunity to step out of the continent of Africa. That, to me, is false expectations, and I think the reverse is true to a greater extent.

Most women love men who make jokes, that is, men who are funny. So when a funny man comes to marry them, they quickly accept, saying to themselves, *He will keep me happy all the time.* They bury themselves in this one characteristic, forgetting other important things. He may be funny but very difficult to understand, uncaring, or very crafty and self-centered. To think you will always be happy in your marriage is nothing but false expectations.

People may meet in a nightclub and later decide to get married. In your mind, you may think he will always take you to the nightclub where he met you. This is nothing but false expectations. He may never allow you to go the nightclub again.

"I will change him or her when we get marry." This is a dangerous trap, and many girls have fallen into it. By the special grace of God, you have known that he is very hard, very wicked, and uncompromising, yet you say you will marry him, hoping you can change him. Is this not just crazy? Human beings have no power to change lives. It is the work of the Holy Spirit, not ours. Some may change, but many will not, leaving the spouse hoping for change confused. If you do not love him or her, do not get married, hoping love will come after, for it may never. Unrealistic expectations are the back door through which all kinds of troubles enter your marriage. And it is the door that can lead to divorce.

Marital Unfaithfulness

Marital unfaithfulness, or infidelity, leads to divorce and is probably the most damaging thing happening to African marriages in the diaspora. It is also one of the most painful problems African married couples face. Almost all the killings we read about in chapter 1 happened because of marital unfaithfulness. The causes of infidelity are numerous and can be simple and, at the same time, very complicated. Let it be made crystal clear that affairs occur in both happy and unhappy marriages, and both spouses are responsible for the situation.

The causes of marital unfaithfulness include low self-esteem; lack of love, attention, and affection given to a spouse; anger; boredom; marrying too young; peer pressure; opportunity; disappointment in the marriage; sex addiction; and a desire to leave the marriage.

Men react to the news of their wives cheating on them differently than women do when they hear their husbands have been unfaithful. It is painful knowing that your husband is cheating, but nothing makes a man helpless, lonely, and humiliated like knowing his wife cheated on him with another man. Sometimes he feels as if he will never get over the stress. It is more stressful for the man when he forces his wife to tell him the details of the affair. No one, man or woman, has the right to be unfaithful. The consequences are unbearable. If you have had an extramarital affair or are thinking of having one, stop and think about the consequences. The effects can haunt you and your family for decades. "But a man who commits adultery lacks judgment; whoever does so destroys himself. Blows and disgrace are his lot, and his shame will never be wiped away" (Proverbs 6: 32-33). Thank God it is a forgivable sin, and this is the time for you to confess and turn from this satanic behavior. If not, God will expose you very soon. You cannot hide it for long. Confess, and all will be well with your soul.

I am not saying you should tell your spouse you cheated. You do not have to announce it on a TV program. You do not have to give a testimony about your old life of cheating in the church. To me, unless you know with certainty the Holy Spirit is leading you to do so, it is not necessary to tell your spouse of your infidelity. I know you can become clean as you present yourself before God in your private prayer of confession. I also do not believe in the saying "Once a cheater always a cheater." We teach and preach for change, and many who used to cheat are transformed by the renewal of their minds through the work of God's grace in their lives, and they do not cheat again.

Bad Company

"Show me your friends and I will tell you who you are." The Bible says, "Do not be misled: Bad company corrupts good character" (1 Cor. 15:33). Hanging around with men and women who do not care about the health of their marriages and families is dangerous. Elderly African women in the diaspora mislead many young girls brought from Africa by their elderly husbands. These women indoctrinate innocent girls to disobey their elderly husbands, telling them how their lives will be better if they seek their independence from those who brought them to the diaspora. They compare their husbands with men who have better homes and cars, and with better paying jobs. They also point to others who have divorced their husbands and now move around almost half-naked as happy, sexy, moneymaking, independent women. You do not have to compare your spouse with other men or women. Use your judgment, and do not walk in the counsel of the wicked. Do not sit at the seat of those who say nothing good about your spouse. Bad company will lead you to fire.

Some bad friends in the diaspora terribly misled young girls who left their husbands in Africa. As some of these girls were seriously struggling for their husbands to join them in the diaspora, their bad friends introduced them to some rich and wayward Africans, who helped them with the money they needed only when the women had given themselves sexually to them. They pushed these women to give in. They showed them other women who supposedly went down the same path and easily brought their families to the diaspora. When their husbands came to the diaspora, these bad women told their friends' husbands how unfaithful their wives had been. This is what bad company can do. They kill you from both ends, giving you no chance to survive.

CHAPTER 6

How to Rescue African Marriages
in the Diaspora

Proposing ways to rescue African marriages in the diaspora is like trying to get tears from a crocodile or trying to skin an ant. In the diaspora, everyone is a king. Even kings will seek advice, but not so with the diaspora kings. Everybody knows everything. Everybody does what he or she likes with his or her life and family. They are gods and goddesses, financially able to do and undo. They are very complicated beings out here in the diaspora. Though many of them talk like white people in their minds, they think like an old man in the village. Some have no moral values in their ways. Many are drowning in the concept of Western freedom, in need of help yet not willing to be helped. Wandering in their pride, yet not willing to ask for help.

The woman feeling so empowered in America says to her husband, "Go to the kitchen, and get your food. Your mother is not here to serve you food. There is no house girl or house help here. After all, we are equals in the diaspora. I pay the bills, too."

Many project happiness, but beneath, there is pain that they try to hide like a young girl in the village, struggling to hide her pregnancy, or someone trying to hide signs of leprosy. Even though all these things are going on, let me humbly present what I believe may be of help to those who would like to try them in their lives and marriages.

Make an Unconditional Decision to Have a Happy Marriage
Marriage may be described like a house with foundation, walls, and roof. You may have a strong marital foundation, but if the walls of your marriage are not built with the right material, it will not be a happy one. As I said earlier, Hollywood has

proven to us in the diaspora that money and fame does not necessarily build a happy marriage. We have also discovered that being in the diaspora is not a panacea for a happy marriage relationship. When some of us were still in Africa, we thought our marriages would be better, full of happiness, and void of stains and wrinkles the moment we stepped in the diaspora. But the reverse is true.

I have heard some couples say, "If only we had children in this marriage, just one, our marriage would have been a happy one." You and I know thousands of marriages full of children, yet bitterness and unhappiness fill them. It takes two people to build a happy marriage, with or without children, with or without money, in the diaspora or Africa. It is an unconditional decision to build a happy marital relationship. It takes time and hard labor to build a happy marriage. Only a fool will destroy what he or she is happy with. If there is no happiness, work on having it in your marriage.

Make a Decision to Love Your Wife
Many African men who come from nations where tribal lines are very visible find it hard to love their wives if they are from a different tribe, as the Bible says they should. African men married to girls from their tribes (but where family lineage is very strong) find it very difficult to love their wives as the Bible says. Many African men love their sisters more than their wives, while others love their mothers more than their wives. Major decisions are made over the phone with siblings and parents back home. The wife may be informed after some time. Ask an African man "your wife and your mother who do you love most and whom will you die for?" Many African men would die for their mothers and sisters but never for their wives. One African musician says "you can have another wife, but you can not have another mother." But the Bible says that the man should love his wife as Christ loved the church and died for. Remember that in the Bible, we are given no room to hate. So the Bible is not saying we should hate any body. When it comes to marriage, God does not want any thing, any person to come inbetween the husband and his wife.

When I talk about love, I am talking about an action, not a word. Instead of saying, "I love you," show your wife by actions that you love her. Many African marriages in the diaspora fail because African men struggle with boxes of chocolates and flowers as a means of showing love. The chocolates may make your wife fat, while the flowers will wither and dry up within days. Some struggle with words like "honey" and "baby." But all these words do not last long. Who cannot do these things? Loving your wife without any reservation is a wonderful decision.

Happy is the man who loves his wife as he loves himself.

> Husbands, love your wives, just as Christ loved the church and gave himself up for her to make her holy, cleansing her by the washing with water through the word, and to present her to himself as a radiant church, without stain or wrinkle or any other blemish, but holy and blameless. In this same way, husbands ought to love their wives as their own bodies. He who loves his wife loves himself. (Eph. 5:25-28)

Love is not everything in marriage, but it is indispensable in all relationships, especially marriage. My wife and I have gone through good and bad times in our marriage. We deeply love each other, and even though love has not prevented our marriage from having issues, it has kept us on track. Our love for each other has not solved our arguments, but it has given us patience to work through them. Our love has not ensured one of us to be always right, but love has given us and will give you the perspective to understand that being right is not always important. Our love for each other has not stopped us from saying hurtful things, but love requires a heartfelt apology. Our love for each other has not made any of us, especially me, to be less annoyed by little things, but love has helped us and will help you to focus on what really matters. Love has not protected us from getting hurt, but love allows us to forgive each other all the time.

Make no mistake about love. Love is not a mystery. You can do specific things with your spouse in order to have a successful marriage. Love that is able to keep a marriage strong and stable is never passive or just a spontaneous experience. It has never "just happened" to anyone, and it will not be you. You have to be determined to love day in and day out. He who loves his wife has no black or red book in which he records the wrongs of his wife, for love keeps no record of wrongdoing.

Make a Decision to Be Submissive to Your Husband

The modern woman living in a modern or postmodern world finds this Bible teaching irrelevant in her world. To her, the teaching is old school, a teaching meant for stay-at-home, uneducated, unproductive, helpless women who depended on the mercies of heartless men in a male-dominated world. Many so-called modern women would rather cut off their husbands' genitals than be submissive to them. Surprisingly, many of these women claim to be Christians. There is no doubt the Lord teaches that a Christian wife is to be submissive to her husband.

The Bible also carries several teachings on this subject of submission: submission to father and mother (Eph. 6:1-3), submission to authorities (Rom. 13:1-7), submission to God (James 4:7), and submission to elders (1 Pet. 5:5).

Submission in these areas is much easier. Power requires us to submit, and age carries authority. In the West, who really cares these days? Children wait to turn eighteen in order to have the right to reject their father's or mother's authority over them. To some, only the need for the almighty dollar makes them submit to their bosses in their workplaces.

A husband has no authority to make his wife submit, either by the Bible or the law, no matter the bride price he paid. The woman has to submit because of devotion. As a Christian wife, her first devotion is to God. Marriage has its rules, which are that the two become one with the husband as the head. And as the leader, he has to love his wife, and the wife has to submit to her husband in Christ. This does not mean the woman has no voice in her home or has no influence on how the family should be managed.

To be submissive does not mean she accepts everything the husband says or that she is less important. Submission is a command, and one has to make a personal choice to obey. The husband is not more important than the woman in any way. In Christ, both the husband and his wife are saved by grace through faith. One has no privilege over the other. But so far as the peace of the family is concerned, and so far as the family would have to reflect the relationship between Christ and his church, this divine principle must be maintained.

When it came to the point of taking the infant baby Jesus Christ to Egypt so King Herod would not kill him, God spoke to Joseph, the head of the family. I am not saying God cannot speak through the woman, because it's clear the Bible is the voice of God, speaking to men and women. A wise man listens to his wife, as well as a wise woman submits to her husband. The woman may be smarter and more hardworking than her husband, making all the money and paying the bills. Thank God you are just as precious as the precious woman in Proverbs 31:10-31. She did everything for her family and never complained, undermined the leadership role of her husband, or refused to be submissive to her husband because she was doing everything. In fact, this woman seemed more hardworking than any woman I have ever seen or heard of.

A wife of noble character who can find? She is worth far more than rubies. Her husband has full confidence in her and lacks nothing of value. She brings him good, not harm, all the days of her life. She selects wool and flax and works with eager hands. She is like the merchant ships, bringing her food from afar. She gets up while it is still night; she provides food for her family and portions for her female servants. She considers a field and buys it; out of her earnings she plants a vineyard. She sets about her work vigorously; her arms are strong for her tasks. She sees that her trading is profitable, and her lamp does not go out at night. In her hand she holds the distaff and grasps the spindle with her fingers. She opens her arms to the poor and extends her hands to the needy. When it snows, she has no fear for her household; for all of them are clothed in scarlet. She makes coverings for her bed; she is clothed in fine linen and purple. Her husband is respected at the city gate, where he takes his seat among the elders of the land. She makes linen garments and sells them, and supplies the merchants with sashes. She is clothed with strength and dignity; she can laugh at the days to come. She speaks with wisdom, and faithful instruction is on her tongue. She watches over the affairs of her household and does not eat the bread of idleness. Her children arise and call her blessed; her husband also, and he praises her: "Many women do noble things, but you surpass them all."

Charm is deceptive, and beauty is fleeting; but a woman who fears the Lord is to be praised. Honor her for all that her hands have done, and let her works bring her praise at the city gate. (Prov. 31:10-31)

Many women reject the idea of submission, because all they have seen and heard about worldly leadership is oppression and domination of others. Biblical leadership, which God wants man to demonstrate in his family, is that of service and servanthood.

Romans 12:2 needs to take place in our lives, so we may be able to enjoy the will of God in submission. "Do not conform to the pattern of this world, but be transformed by the renewing of your mind. Then you will be able to test and approve what God's will is—his good, pleasing and perfect will."

Worldly and unregenerated men, together with our human tradition, have abused the concept of a woman's submissiveness to her husband. Today, worldly women all over the world promise freedom to other women, telling them not to be submissive to their husbands, for men and women are equal and women are even better. They do not have the freedom they are professing. "They promise them freedom, while they themselves are slaves of depravity" (2 Pet. 2:19a).

There is no freedom to whoever tries to alter the way God, in his sovereignty, has made things to be. A fish can only be free in water, not on the land. Do not stand afar and say that being submissive to one's husband is a sign of weakness. Taste it, and you will enjoy it. "Taste and see that the Lord is good" (Ps. 34:8a).

Women who have decided to be submissive to their husbands for the glory of God enjoy their families and marriages, while those who have chosen not to submit have destroyed themselves and ruined their homes. A husband who loves the Lord, one who loves his wife as Christ loved and died for the church, will remain restless when he fails to do what his submissive wife has said. The reverse is true for a woman who is not submissive to her husband.

Make a Decision to Be Forgiving

- "Forgiveness is not an elective in the curriculum of servant hood. It is a required course, and the exams are always tough to pass" (Charles Swindoll).
- "The most crucial issue in a marriage is not that couples communicate, but what they communicate. Let the thing communicated be forgiveness" (Walter Wangerin Jr.).
- "Forgiveness is powerful and beneficial. When we forgive someone for hurting us, it frees us from feeling like victims or feeling we are under the power of the person who hurt us" (Grace Ketterman and Kathy King).
- "If you forget, you will not forgive at all. You can never forgive people for things you have forgotten" (Lewis Smedes).
- "The best remedy for painful memories is not forgetting the offense, but remembering your decision to forgive. If you are going to remember a wrong, make sure you also remember how you dealt with the wrong" (Robert Jeffress).

- "Forgiveness is the oil that lubricates family relationships and nowhere is it more needed than among sibling" (David and Claudia).
- "All marriage authorities say the same thing. A healthy marriage is one in which forgiveness is practiced. To develop a closer relationship it is vital to give forgiveness but also receive forgiveness with grace" (Jim and Cathy).
- "Therefore, if you are offering your gift at the altar and there remember that your brother has something against you, leave your gift there in front of the altar. First go and be reconciled to your brother; then come and offer your gift" (Matt. 5:23-24).
- "Be kind to one another, tenderhearted, forgiving one another, as God in Christ forgave you" (Eph. 4:32).
- "And whenever you stand praying, forgive, if you have anything against anyone, so that your Father also who is in heaven may forgive you your trespasses" (Mark 11:25).
- "Then Peter came to Jesus and asked, 'Lord, how many times shall I forgive my brother when he sins against me? Up to seven times?' Jesus answered, 'I tell you, not seven times, but seventy-seven times'" (Matt. 18:21-22).
- "While they were stoning him, Stephen prayed, 'Lord Jesus, receive my spirit.' Then he fell on his knees and cried out, 'Lord, do not hold this sin against them.' When he had said this, he fell asleep" (Acts 7:59-60).
- "Anyone whom you forgive, I also forgive. What I have forgiven, if I have forgiven anything, has been for your sake in the presence of Christ, so that we would not be outwitted by Satan; for we are not ignorant of his designs" (2 Cor. 2:10-11).

An unforgiving spirit is dangerous. When you hold a grudge or store unforgiveness against your spouse in your heart, you jeopardize your own health.

An unforgiving spirit creates things like anger, a judgmental spirit, criticism, resentment, and so forth. These harbored emotions are like toxins in the body that create stress and can lead to illness and perhaps in extreme cases, like the killing of your spouse mercilessly, as we see among Africans today in the diaspora.

Unforgiving feelings affect us mentally, physically, and spiritually. It also affects our day-to-day activities and our interactions with people. Are you keeping anything against your spouse in your heart? Why imprison yourself? If you forgive, you will have fresh air in your life and family.

Make a Decision Not to Be Angry

- "Anger is like a homemade bomb strapped around one's waist. Whoever detonates the bomb becomes a suicide bomber. They not only injure anyone in the near vicinity but they go up as well. Anger destroys their reputation, devastated friendships and worst of all amputates their potential" (Wayne Cordeiro).

- "When anger is the rule in a person's life, the spirits of hate, malice, resentment. bitterness, jealously, rage and the like are drawn to it like flies are drawn to honey" (Eddie and Alice Smith).

- "Speaking in anger is classified as careless because when we speak in anger we are not thinking of the consequences of our words" (Rhonda Rizzo Webb).

- "Now the works of the flesh are evident: sexual immorality, impurity, sensuality, idolatry, sorcery, enmity, strife, jealousy, fits of anger, rivalries, dissensions, divisions, envy, drunkenness, orgies, and things like these. I warn you, as I warned you before, that those who do such things will not inherit the kingdom of God" (Gal. 5:19-21).

- "Be angry and do not sin; do not let the sun go down on your anger, and give no opportunity to the devil. Let the thief no longer steal, but rather let him labor, doing honest work with his own hands, so that he may have something to share with anyone in need" (Eph. 4:26-28).

- "But now you must put them all away: anger, wrath, malice, slander, and obscene talk from your mouth. Put on then, as God's chosen ones, holy and beloved, compassionate hearts, kindness, humility, meekness, and patience, bearing with one another and, if one has a complaint against another, forgiving each other; as the Lord has forgiven you, so you also must forgive" (Col. 3:8, 12-13).

- "But for Cain and his offering he the Lord had no regard. So Cain was very angry, and his face fell. The Lord said to Cain, 'Why are you angry, and why has your face fallen? If you do well, will you not be accepted? And if you do not do well, sin is crouching at the door. Its desire is for you, but you must rule over it.' Cain spoke to Abel his brother. And when they were in the field, Cain rose up against his brother Abel and killed him" (Gen. 4:5-8).

- "Refrain from anger, and forsake wrath. Fret not yourself; it tends only to evil" (Ps. 37:8).

- "A hot-tempered man stirs up strife, but he who is slow to anger quiets contention" (Prov. 15:18).
- "A man of wrath stirs up strife, and one given to anger causes much transgression" (Prov. 29:22).
- "For pressing milk produces curds, pressing the nose produces blood, and pressing anger produces strife" (Prov. 30:33).

Chapter 1 reveals that anger caused all the killings recorded in the reports. No matter how deeply you may think your spouse has hurt you, I think that getting angry to whatever level is a choice we all make. I have seen this in my own relationship with my wife and my friends. Sometimes I choose to be angry; other times, I find myself smiling over it and letting it pass, choosing not to be angry. I do not think I am the only human being who experiences this. If anger is a time bomb, we should all run away from it. Why should you be angry to the point of killing your spouse and going to jail? You can still make it in life, with or without her or him. Letting her go with all the humiliation you think she has brought you is not a sign of weakness but of greatness and true manliness. Killing her and yourself is nothing but lack of self-control and a false belief that she is all of your life or the anchor of your life. Killing your wife and going to jail for cheating on you, filing for divorce, or whatever reason is not smart. It is said that the downfall of a man is not the end of his life. Whenever you come to these dark points in life, know you have two options before you: to be angry and not to be angry.

After reading this book, I pray you will say to yourself, *I will never choose to be driven by anger and bitterness to the point of killing a human being or doing any foolish thing that is not manly.* Choose to smile and let her go in peace, a sign of greatness and maturity.

Make a Decision to Be Committed to Your Spouse

Commitment, not attraction, is the foundation of a lifelong happy marriage. Commitment in marriage is the couple's dedication to one another. This dedication focuses on their relationship as well as in their happiness as a couple. Commitment gives a couple the strength and courage to go through bad times together, sharing a common vision to remain married whatever happens. A marital relationship is not always as sweet as some will daydream. Commitment keeps marriages together when, along the way, familiarity and other marital complications make you seem to think the other partner is less attractive.

Commitment in marriage is very important. All who recognize the importance of marriage in the building of a strong community and a happy marriage highly value it. Commitment is seen in all the Bible says about marriage. "For this reason a man will leave his father and mother and be united to his wife and they will become one flesh" (Gen. 2:24). The decision to commit your life to your spouse is a once-and-for-all decision. Jesus said, "Therefore, what God has joined together, let man not separate" (Matt. 19:6).

Commitment is required in a marital relationship in which a man and woman desire to enjoy a sense of union and freedom. Commitment is a decision to live together as husband and wife made well before the man and women ever go before a judge, pastor, or priest to recite marriage vows. The decision is made on the knees, or any posture, in the most private place, which is your heart in prayer, alone with your God. It is renewed each step of the way. Commitment to Christ makes commitment to marriage stronger.

As you drive around, attend meetings, and go to work, meeting and interacting with women who seem more beautiful and ready to give you everything, even themselves, tell yourself, *I am committed to one woman, and I will keep the commitment, come rain or shine.*

Sometimes you feel tempted to try a white woman and gratify your sinful nature, but you tell yourself, *I am committed to my black women, my wife black or white and I am content with her. Our women go through the same stuff.* What keeps a woman faithful to her husband is her commitment to him, even when another man promises her heaven on earth.

The cost of commitment could be the most significant reason so many Africans in the diaspora choose not to marry and why married ones find it difficult to remain married. Many African marriages in the diaspora lack commitment. You can make the decision now to be committed to your marriage and your spouse. It is a personal decision, and those who make it end up really enjoying their marriages. The cost of commitment may be high, but the benefits are higher.

Make a Decision to Be Tolerant

Tolerance in marriage is experienced and learned as the couple grows together. You need tolerance, because there are times when you need to be patient and not argue. Though there are times when you have to make your opinions known, there are times when only silence can do the job.

You do not always have to shout, "This cup should not be here." "The toilet seat has pee on it." "Who did this?" The bed should be made." "You put your socks here again." You say you do not like the smell of alcohol, but he comes home drunk again and again, and he wants you to kiss him. You do not smoke, but he gets up in the middle of the night and smokes in the bedroom. You need to learn how to respond to such things.

In marriage, there will be many times when very little things will make you not understand your spouse. You may even become frustrated with talking about the same thing repeatedly. The only way out is tolerance and patience. When you experience anger out of frustration, you may not be exercising enough patience with the situations around you. You do not have to tolerate your spouse, but remember we all make mistakes, and we all have our good and bad days. If you are a perfectionist and do not understand in this manner, marriage may not be the best institution for you.

Tolerance and patience are virtues that are to be practiced in all marriages. It does not matter how much you love your spouse, your patience and character will be tried at times. A healthy marriage requires a great deal of effort and tolerance. Without the effort of both spouses, your marriage will soon begin to backfire. Still, you do not have to sacrifice the moral values of your life and family and your faith in the Lord Jesus Christ on the altar of tolerance.

Praying Together
It is said that the family that prays together stays together. And a praying family is a happy one. Through prayers, several family issues are handled. A praying family honors the lordship of Christ and lives in accordance with biblical values. This family has Christ as its foundation, and God the creator is their family God.

> But if serving the Lord seems undesirable to you, then choose for yourselves this day whom you will serve, whether the gods your forefathers served beyond the River, or the gods of the Amorites, in whose land you are living. But as for me and my household, we will serve the Lord. (Josh. 24:15)

- Prayer is a conversation with God. God speaks to us through his Holy Word while we talk with him through prayers. Through prayers, we cast our marriage and family cares unto the Lord.

- "Prayer is the greatest power God has put into our hands for service" (Mary Slessor).
- "When we work, we work, but when we pray, God works. His supernatural strength is available to praying people who are convinced to the core of their beings that he can make a difference" (Bill Hybel).
- "The devil smiles when we are up working, but he trembles when we pray" (Corrie ten Boom).
- "Prayer brings momentum. It lifts the heart above the challenges of life and gives it a view of God's resources of victory and hope. Prayer may not change all things for you but it sure changes you for all things" (John Mason).
- "Prayer is a declaration of our dependence on God. It isn't something mechanical you do, it is somewhere you go to meet someone you know" (Jill Briscoe).
- "The very thing that qualifies us to pray is our helplessness" (David Jeremiah).
- "Make no decision without prayer" (Elizabeth George).
- "When all other courses of action have been eliminated, when we stand on the edge of the abyss when we approach God with empty hands and an aching heart, then we draw close to the true heart of prayer" (Jerry Sittser).
- "The prayer of a Christian is not an attempt to force God's hands, but a humble acknowledgment of our helplessness and dependence" (J. I. Packer).

Who says that he or she is not helpless when it comes to the point of marriage and family? Who is the man who knows how to truly handle a woman without any help? Who is the woman who says she knows her husband so well that she needs no help? Tell me the family that truly knows how to bring up children in the Lord in these days and age without any prayers.

The decision to marry your spouse, if it was rightly done, was done in prayers. Prayer will sustain the decision throughout this life. Pray you do not fall into temptations. Temptation is very common to all husbands and all wives. Why not pray for your neighbors and friends? If you do not like something in your marriage, take it to God in prayers. If there is any fight to fight, why not fight it with God, not your spouse? Instead of all-night talking and a nightly war of words with your spouse, why not have a night vigil with God about the issues troubling your marriage and family? If you have to fast and pray, do it with wisdom. I came across a woman who said she abstained from sex for a year, because she and her husband had lots of spiritual battles to fight. As she did, another woman took her husband away, and she now struggles with her children alone. She feels she was doing the right thing, but I think she was crazy.

It is also very painful to say that great prayer warriors who left Africa burning with zeal and passion for spiritual things become as cold as ice the moment they set their feet in the diaspora. Work and money sucked all their passion and love for the Lord. They work on Sundays, and they deceive themselves with the belief that, if they do not work on weekends, they will have no jobs.

The husband and wife have no time to pray together and no personal time of prayer with the Lord. If you have spent time in Africa serving the Lord, be sure that, in the diaspora, Satan will do everything to kill your spirit, destroy your marriage, and put you in spiritual misery. Wherever you are, do not play with prayers. The pleasures and pressures of life are too much for the families. Families and marriages are becoming worthless in the diaspora. Satan is very active in the diaspora, seeking families and marriages to destroy. May it not be your family or your marriage. Pray and pray always.

Trust and Keep the Trust
The thinking by many women that men cannot be trusted and that if your husband is handsome, you should be prepared to share him with other women is not healthy for marriage. Men say the same thing about their beautiful wives. This thinking does not build trust. Instead, it builds suspicion, which leads to the spouse checking each other's phone, e-mail, and Facebook page. When he or she talks with someone of the opposite sex for some time, the other partner starts saying he or she is having an affair. Unfounded, baseless, and senseless suspicions have caused some couples to foolishly do what their partners accused them of doing.

Any marriage void of trust is headed toward or may already be in an abusive relationship. Trust is the most important ingredient of a relationship. It gives flavor to an intimate relationship between husband and wife. Trust, like other virtues, does not just appear in a marriage. The couple has to cultivate and nurture it. It takes years to establish trust in a relationship, but a single act of unfaithfulness can destroy everything. Trust has to be established before the man and woman decide to marry.

These things will help establish trust before and during your marriage.

Transparency
A transparent relationship is an open and free exchange of information. This means you will have to share information with your spouse about your activities, your daily

life, and your plans for the future. The motto of transparency in a marriage relation is, "Nothing to hide." If you leave your jobsite and have to stop somewhere with a friend, call your spouse, and tell him or her where you are and the person you are with. I know most African men do not feel comfortable with this idea. To them, it is as if they are asking permission from their wives to be where they want to be. Telling your wife where you are does not reduce your position as a husband. The more you are open to each other, the happier your marriage becomes. Showing your spouse your paycheck and how the money is spent helps you and the family. If you cannot tell your spouse everything about your business, there may be no trust, and there is no transparency.

Reliability
Couples have to work to present themselves as reliable to each other. You cannot depend on an unreliable person. You are reliable when you keep your promises, when your yes is yes and your no is no, but not blind to life circumstances. When you are caring and giving your spouse a sense of comfort and when you show positive consistency and stability in all your ways.

Honesty
Honesty is of utmost importance in establishing and maintaining a strong marriage. Honesty allows you to build trust in each other. Transparency, honesty, and reliability go hand in hand, and if you don't have them, you will find it very difficult to have a joyful marriage.

Trust is very delicate and can be broken in so many ways and the most common ways are—an affair, hidden addictions, little lies here and there, and financial secrecy—can break it. Something is wrong with trust when you cannot answer your spouse's phone and read your spouse's letters.

If trust is broken in your marriage, you have to give your spouse a chance to reestablish the broken trust he or she once had in you. It is easy to forgive, but it takes time to rebuild trust. Make sure you do not betray the trust your spouse has in you.

Apply Delilah's Charm in Your Marriage
Do not come to a conclusion yet. Do not tell me the Bible says that charm is deceitful. I know this will be a surprise to many people. To many, any person with the name Delilah is evil. One day, I was watching a TV program with my sons. A singing group

called Delilah came up to sing. My boys could not believe why the group was named after an evil woman. When the group sang, my little boys and I were moved and wished the Delilah group qualified for the final round of the singing competition. What I call Delilah's charm is the ability she used to bring down mighty Samson.

The Bible says women are the weaker vessels or partners. The same Bible says, "Let the weak say they are strong" (1 Peter 3:7; Joel 3:10). Delilah was very smart and knew God had adorned her with natural charm that would subdue a man. The Bible does not say Delilah used any spell to subdue Samson. We are not told that she visited a witch doctor to get powers to overcome Samson. She used only her natural, God-given charm, and every woman has her natural charm. Though Delilah used her own charm negatively, you can learn from her and use yours positively. The woman out there on the street who is pulling your husband from you may be using what you have refused to use: your natural charm.

No doubt the Bible says the sons of this world are more clever than the sons of light (Luke 16:8). It can also be said that the daughters of this world are more clever than the daughters of light. Let us find out what Delilah's charm is.

The Charm of the Comfort of Her Home

Delilah made her home a comfortable place. Delilah charmed Samson with comfort. Whenever Samson went out, he rushed back home. The Bible does not tell us how long Samson was with Delilah, but I know it took some time after each effort that Delilah made to know Samson's secret. Samson found comfort only in Delilah's home. How comfortable have you made your home? Many husbands choose to be away from home, because their wives have chased comfort out of their homes. May you not be one of those women. Men are also called to make their homes comfortable for their wivies. Why should your presence at home make your wife uneasy? Why should she always feel sick when she is on her way home or when she knows you will soom be coming home? Comfort brings life, happiness and peace in a marriage.

Availability

She made herself available to Samson all the times. When there is a little misunderstanding, our women in the diaspora drive out when their husbands come home. Some will chat on the Internet for endless hours. Others will remain on the phone, calling one friend after the other, while the husband looks for something to eat. After all, we are in the diaspora. Any woman who chooses this path of not being available to her husband all the time works against herself.

Calmness

Delilah did not get angry. Nor did she abuse Samson or refuse to give him food after the first and second failures. She did not command Samson. She was calm, showing no signs of bitterness and danger or evil intention. The problem with some of our women today is that, with any little thing, they are already talking at the top of their voices. They cut off communication so easily. With a humble spirit, Delilah communicated what she wanted. And she got it.

Laps

Delilah knew the power of a woman's lap. Her lap was her charm. Is there any woman who has no lap? It does not matter how big or how small your lap may be. In that lap of yours, God has put unspeakable charm for your joy and the comfort of your husband. Today there are fake ladies lap pillaws in the market for lonely men and many are rushing for these fake ladies lap pillaws designed in Japan. This should help us understand the importance of a woman's lap to almost all men. The Bible says Delilah put Samson's head on her lap. He slept so deeply on that lap to the extent that she shaved his hair without him feeling it. On Delilah's lap, the giant slept like a baby. Can you remember when your husband last slept on your lap? If you have a lap, know it has comforting power. Know that there is real consolation vibrating from that lap. Use your charm and your lap in building yourself a happy home and a happy marriage for the glory of God.

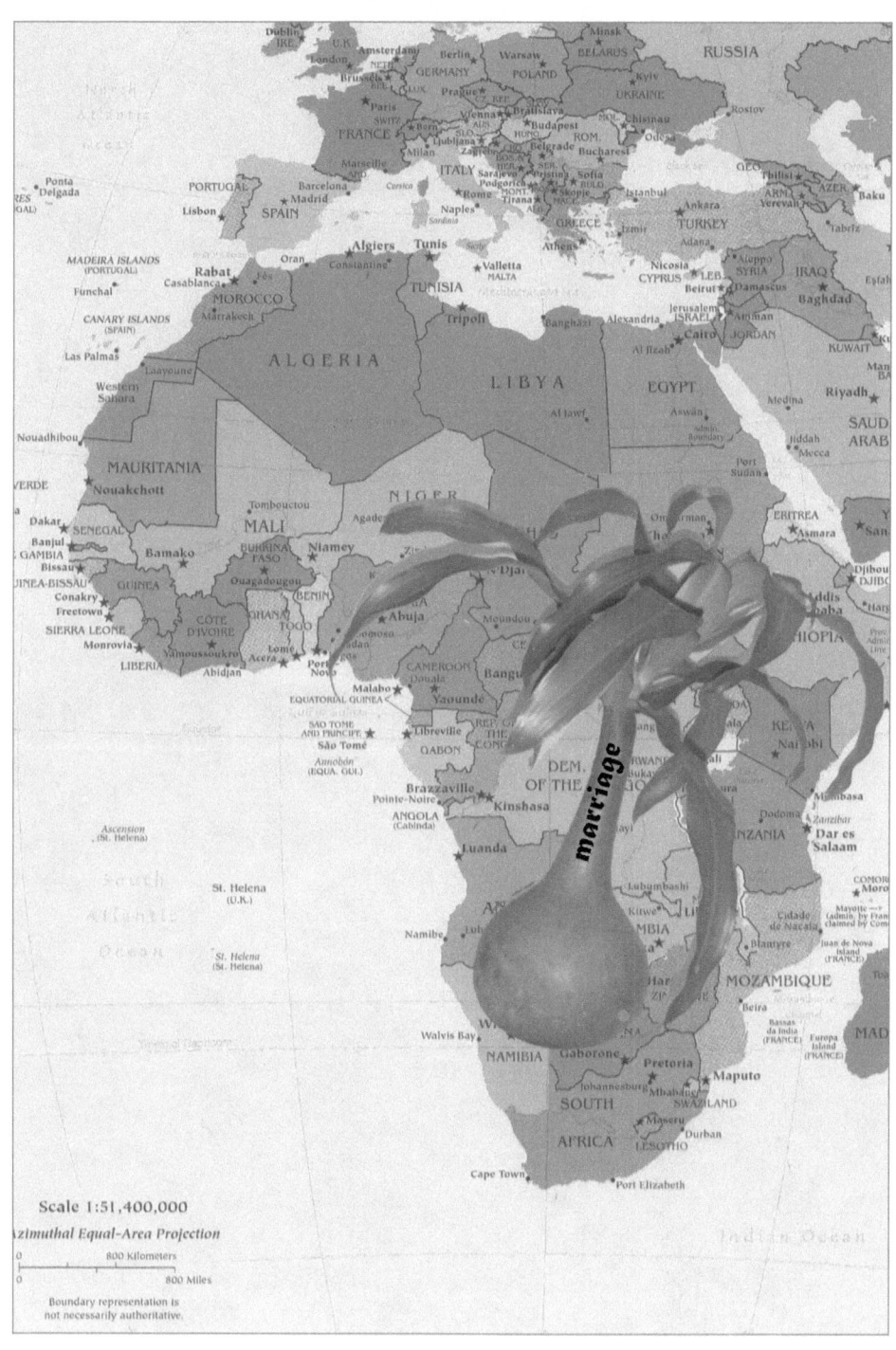

God, against all odds help me to keep my marriage upright.

Conclusion

After having said almost everything humanly possible about rescuing African marriages in the diaspora, I want to say there is hope for any struggling marriage. After I have said all I believe I have been led to say concerning African marriages in the diaspora, I want to say there is a way out, and Jesus is the only way out. He is also the only way to a happy marriage.

If your marriage is in trouble, needing to be rescued, Jesus is the best and perfect rescuer of sinking marriages. He can calm the storms of life being thrown against your marriage.

If Jesus must rescue your marriage, you must do what he asks you to do. You need to cooperate with the rescuer. Jesus would first want you to hand over your life to him, together with the leadership of your marriage. This is how he functions. Put aside your evil ambitions and pride, and listen to the Lord.

What causes fights and quarrels in your marriage? Don't they come from your desires that battle within you? You desire but do not have, so you kill. You covet but cannot get what you want, so you quarrel and fight. You do not have because you do not ask God. When you ask, you do not receive, because you ask with the wrong motives, such as to spend what you get on your pleasures.

You adulterous people, don't you know that friendship with the world means enmity against God? Therefore, anyone who chooses to be a friend of the world becomes an enemy of God. Or do you think Scripture says without reason that he jealously longs for the spirit he has caused to dwell in us? But he gives us more grace. That is why Scripture says, "God opposes the proud but shows favor to the humble."

Submit yourselves, then, to God. Resist the devil, and he will flee from you. Come near to God and he will come near to you. Wash your hands, you sinners, and purify your hearts, you double-minded. Grieve, mourn and wail. Change your laughter to mourning and your joy to gloom. Humble yourselves before the Lord, and he will lift you up. (James 4:1-10)

The Lord bless you and keep you; the Lord make his face shine on you and be gracious to you; the Lord turn his face toward you and give you peace. (Num. 6:24-26)

Amen.

Bibliography

Chapman, Gary. *The Four Seasons of Marriage*. Wheaton, Ill.: Tyndale House Publishers, Inc., 2005.

—. *The Marriage You've Always Wanted*. Chicago: Moody Publishers, 2005.

Cordeiro, Wayne. *Spiritual House Cleaning*. Ventura, Calif.: The Dream Releasers, Regal Books, 2002.

Daley, Jerome, and Kellie Daley. *Not Your Parents' Marriage*. Colorado Springs: Waterbrook Press, 2006.

Flanigan, Beverly. *Forgiving the Unforgivable*. New York: Wiley Publishing, Inc., 1992.

Gehman, J. Richard. *African Traditional Religion*. Nyeri, Kenya: Kesho Publications, 1990.

Horsley, Call Gloria. *The In-Law Survival Manual*. New York: John Wiley & Sons, Inc., 1997.

Hybels, Bill. *Too Busy Not to Pray*. Westmont, Ill.: InterVarsity Books, 1988.

Kotin, Joel. *How to Change Your Spouse and Save Your Marriage*. Franklin Lakes, N.J.: The Career Press, Inc., 2001.

MacArthur, John, Jr. *Alone with God*. Colorado Springs: David Cook, 1995.

Mason, John. *The Impossible Is Possible*. Bloomington, Minn.: Bethany House Publishers, 2003.

Meinecke, Christine. *Everybody Marries the Wrong Person*. Far Hills, N.J.: New Horizon Press, 2010.

Munroe, Myles. *The Purpose and Power of Love & Marriage*. Shippensburg, Pa.: Destiny Image Publishers, Inc., 2002.

Parkman, M Allen. *Smart Marriage*. Westport, Conn.: Praeger Published, 2007.

Parrott, Les, and Leslie Parrott. *Saving Your Marriage Before It Starts*. Grand Rapids, Mich.: Zondervan, 2006.

——. *When Bad Things Happen to Good Marriages*. Grand Rapids, Mich.: Zondervan, 2001.

Smith, Eddie, and Alice Smith. *Spiritual House Cleaning*. Ventura, Calif.: Regal Books, 2003.

Smith, Robin. *Lies at the Altar*. New York: Hyperion, 2006.

Smith, J. Sidney. *Before Saying YES to Marriage*. Santa Barbara, Calif.: Sidney James, 2000.

Sproul, R. C. *The Intimate Marriage*. Phillipsburg, N.J.: P&R Publishing, 2003.

Stoop, David. *Forgiving the Unforgivable*. Ventura, Calif.: Regal Books, 2005.

Wangerin, Walter. *As for Me and My House*. Nashville: Thomas Nelson, 1990.

Webb, Rhonda. *Words Begin in Our Hearts*. Chicago: Moody Publishing, 2003.

www.ingramcontent.com/pod-product-compliance
Lightning Source LLC
Chambersburg PA
CBHW022059170526
45157CB00004B/1405